Why I Am a Pacifist

Why I Am a Pacifist combines personal reflection with a range of historical, philosophical and faith-based insights to give a concise but powerful answer to anyone who thinks that pacifism is about doing nothing in the face of injustice. If you're drawn to pacifism but have doubts and questions, then this book is a good place to start.
Symon Hill, Peace Pledge Union

Tim Gee is wonderfully articulate in this informative, thought-provoking and moving account of why he, along with many other Quakers, is a pacifist.
Chloe Scaling, The Young Quaker magazine

This book is a short, clear, comprehensive explanation of pacifism that covers all the bases and doesn't shy away from the difficult questions. As it moves effortlessly from the theory of a Just War to the practical successes of nonviolent protest, from the origins of pacifism to its links with the struggles against racism and sexism, the book highlights just how essential a peaceful approach is to us and the world.
Oliver Robertson, Fellowship of Reconciliation UK

Following Maria J Stephan's insight that overall nonviolent campaigns are twice as likely to succeed as military ones, in Tim Gee's hands pacifism becomes the ultimate campaign, in the sense that it offers resistance not only to conventional wars but also the violence of poverty and racism, gender based violence and inequality across the globe. Framed by the author's personal reflections, interspersed with insights from the Quaker tradition on equality and peace, this excellent resource will encourage us

to challenge our propensity to violence both as individuals and in our organisations.
Henrietta Cullinan, Catholic Worker

Pacifism is about the whole of life. Read this book to find out why.
Hannah Brock, War Resisters' International

QUAKER QUICKS

Why I Am a Pacifist

QUAKER QUICKS

Why I Am a Pacifist

Tim Gee

CHRISTIAN ALTERNATIVE
BOOKS

Winchester, UK
Washington, USA

JOHN HUNT PUBLISHING

First published by Christian Alternative Books, 2018
Christian Alternative Books is an imprint of John Hunt Publishing Ltd.,
No. 3 East St., Alresford, Hampshire SO24 9EE, UK
office@jhpbooks.com
www.johnhuntpublishing.com
www.christian-alternative.com

For distributor details and how to order please visit the 'Ordering' section on our website.

Text copyright: Tim Gee 2018
Cover photo: Quaker Climate Justice protest at the British Museum

ISBN: 978 1 78904 016 6
978 1 78904 017 3 (ebook)
Library of Congress Control Number: 2018953745

A CIP catalogue record for this book is available from the British Library.

Design: Stuart Davies

UK: Printed and bound by CPI Group (UK) Ltd, Croydon, CR0 4YY
US: Printed and bound by Thomson-Shore, 7300 West Joy Road, Dexter, MI 48130

We operate a distinctive and ethical publishing philosophy in all areas of our business, from our global network of authors to production and worldwide distribution.

Contents

Acknowledgments

Thank you to my friends and family who have read over drafts and given feedback including Marcela, Maria, Paul, Sita, Yvonne, Clive, Chloe, Simon, John, Ahlya, Paul, Till, Oliver, Sasha, Dorothy, Hannah and Jonathan. Thanks also to Friends House library and its ever-helpful staff who helped me locate some of the source material. The cover picture is by Marcela Teran. The series was the idea of Jennifer Kavanagh. All mistakes are of course my own.

Preface

This book is about pacifism written from the perspective of a Quaker. On the basis that you might not have come across Quakers before, this preface attempts some words on the theme.

Quakers (also known as the Religious Society of Friends – or Friends for short) are a grassroots faith community born three and a half centuries ago in the wake of the English Civil War. Quaker ideas are rooted in the principle of equality, especially the experience that every person has the ability to encounter the divine personally. This is represented by the idea of an 'inward light'. Although styles of worship differ around the world, Quaker Meetings are often based on collective contemplation.

The egalitarianism of the community has often led Friends to be pioneers in taking stands that would later become mainstream including promoting women's ministry (1650s), campaigning against slavery (1750s), modelling fair dealing in business (1850s) and challenging homophobia (1950s onwards). Quakers today support programmes to promote environmental protection, economic equality and racial justice amongst other issues.

What Quakers are probably best known for though, is persistently working for peace. That is the focus of the pages that follow.

Chapter 1

Why I am a pacifist

I call myself a pacifist. I haven't always done so and I sometimes hesitate to if I think I might be misunderstood. But with a short book ahead of me to explain what I mean, I say with confidence: I am a pacifist – by which I mean that I try to play my part in making peace by nonviolent means.

Perhaps my pacifism hasn't yet been fully tested. I haven't been a soldier or a resident of a country invaded by another nor been forced in to the military through conscription. Nevertheless, as a resident of a country which drops bombs on other countries, sells weapons to governments engaged in human rights abuse and is complicit in climate change – causing perhaps the largest process of global violence imaginable – I feel a responsibility to speak out and do what I can to work for peace.

I am a pacifist first and foremost because of a profound physiological, psychological and spiritual sense that I couldn't kill another person and that to inflict pain on others is wrong. Different cultures have used different words and explanations for this feeling. Within many world religions and cultures there is a group that feels likewise. In Britain – where I live and grew up – perhaps the best known is the Quaker community of which I am part. I declare my background from the start, and have no doubt my outlook has been shaped by my experience of this community. But true to the non-doctrinal, non-creedal tradition it is also a position I have come to myself.

When approached to write this book, I was asked if I might offer something about campaigning and activism. On reflection, I asked if might explore pacifism instead, precisely because it is the root of why I act. It isn't called 'Why you should be a pacifist' or 'why we should all be pacifists' even though I hope that both you and we all one day will. In the spirit of the idea that we are each engaged on a personal journey, the only truth I can authentically speak to is my own, through my process of action and reflection so far.

How I became a pacifist

I haven't always been a pacifist. I got into a lot of fights at school. I didn't start them. If a fight broke out everyone would leave what they were doing and crowd around to form an improvised boxing ring, cheering the likely victors on. Being a fairly tall person, I could usually hold my own. In so doing, like many other boys, I expressed my schoolyard belief that masculinity relies on the willingness to engage in physical combat.

My friendship group was mostly other boys from the Manchester rock music subculture. Although increasingly sure that I wasn't gay myself, I wasn't experienced enough to be certain. The fact that the artists we admired were often androgynous, and the fact it was OK in our group to be gay, meant that the attacks on us had a strongly homophobic tone: 'Moshers!', 'Homos!', 'Poofs'. And so it continued, right through to the final day. At morning break we went to our hangout place, to find it covered with graffiti. A minute later, some boys whizzed past armed with eggs, which they lobbed in our direction. It was a direct hit on our heads. The insides dribbled down our faces and clothes.

'This is it,' we said. 'That's enough.' We thought that if we didn't do something about this now, we'd never get the chance and it was time to teach them a lesson. So, we piled into an older student's car, skipped the morning's lessons to get showered, then stopped by on the way back to the school to the nearest cash-and-carry to buy as many eggs as we could. At the beginning of lunchtime, we were ready.

Fizzy with nerves we walked up to our assailants' smoking area as calmly as we could and started throwing eggs. As our missiles hit their targets, it was as if an army started charging towards us. Within minutes the entire school yard seemed to have descended into a riot and we turned tail and ran. Punches were raining down on us more than ever before.

We escaped to the car again and drove around the corner, shaking all over and patting one another on the back for our bravery. We stopped at a grass verge where we drew medals on one another's shirts. There was something in that act which affected me. I felt sick to the depths of my stomach, then the sensation washed right over me – perhaps even from beyond me – that what I had done was wrong. Sure, it was only eggs, not stones, not bombs. But nevertheless, I found myself thinking that this is how wars begin. I know now that this realisation would change my life. That was the day I became a pacifist.

I didn't have words for that feeling at that time and I wish I might have found an accessible introductory book to pacifist ideas. Fifteen years later, this reflection is an attempt to fill the gap, in a quest to interpret through writing what began as the instinctive promptings of a heartfelt truth.

What is pacifism?

The word pacifist is not widely understood. Culture shapes language, which in turn shapes the way we think and the decisions we make. That we speak of 'nonviolence' reveals that within our culture, violence is the norm. We do not refer to war as 'nonpeace'.[1]

We do, however, have the word pacifist. Even that, though, has come to be most often defined as what it is not – as a refusal to engage in violence. Sometimes it is intentionally misconstrued as a synonym for passivity, or even pacification. At its root though, pacifism means the act of making peace. As such it describes an active process.

Whilst blurring the meaning of pacifism is sometimes the intention of advocates of war, it does touch on a historic tension, still reflected today in movements for peace. As nonviolence educator David Gee (no relation) explains, we find the root of the English word 'peace' in the Latin word *pax* meaning agreement – in the sense of the word *pact* – and the Indo-European *pag* meaning 'fetter' or 'chain'. Those with an interest in classical history will be familiar with the 'Pax Romana' – an imperial peace without justice imposed by Rome militarily on its empire.

That is not the only way to understand the word though: Also translated into English as 'peace' is the Hebrew word *shalom* and the Arabic *salaam*. This more spiritual sense denotes 'wholeness, abundance, health, wellbeing – the integrity of our common aliveness'. Understood this way a commitment to peace encompasses a commitment to equality, economic justice and environmental protection. In contrast the origin of the word violence is to 'break'.[2]

The introduction of the word 'pacifist' to the English language is often traced to a speech about a system of international arbitration to resolve conflicts given to the universal peace congress of 1910 which spoke of the need for a word to denote work for a positive peace – rather than mere 'anti-war-ism'. In the shadow of the First World War though, popular understanding of the word narrowed to mean mere non-participation in war – the exact definition it had been coined as an alternative to.

I often wish we had a better word. In an online video titled 'Why I Am Not a Pacifist' in the *QuakerSpeak* series, Kristina Keefe-Perry shares how the word 'pacifist' is too small for what she would like it to mean, falling short of the revolutionary possibilities implied in Jesus' teaching against the multifaceted violence of poverty and greed, as well as war.[3] 'Shalomist' and 'pacificist' are amongst the words used to convey shades of variety in approaches to work for peace.[4] Rather than attempting to create a new word though, this book is an attempt to reclaim the word we've got.

To explain why I am a pacifist, I should begin by explaining what I mean by it. When I talk about pacifism I am talking about a commitment to not killing, not supporting killing and trying to undo the systems and structures that lead to killing. It doesn't simply mean going on peace protests every so often, then getting on with business as usual in-between. Even if our actions are imperfect in the present, we can each have a role creating the conditions where peace can thrive. So too it is a commitment to working for justice. Until that time comes we could probably think of the absence of fighting simply as a 'truce' rather than true peace.[5]

This is a pacifism rooted in spirituality, reflected in the words of the best known early Quaker George Fox who declared that he 'lived in the virtue of that life and power that takes away the occasion of all wars'.[6] Already in prison for what we might nowadays call acts of nonviolent civil disobedience, Fox's incarceration was extended for refusing to enlist in the army. In so doing he acted as an inspiration, pattern and example to thousands of Quakers – amongst many others – who have worked, struggled and sometimes suffered for their deeply held conviction that it is wrong to kill.

The Peace Testimony

The Quaker commitment to work for peace is usually traced to the 1660s. As the story goes, Quaker leader Margaret Fell rode by horseback from Cumbria to London where she petitioned the king not to oppress the still nascent movement. The document she presented declared the Society of Friends 'a people that follow after those things that make for peace, love and unity'; and who 'bear our testimony against all strife, and wars and contentions that come from the lusts that war in the members, that war in the soul'.[7] From those early days onwards, Friends have seen war as a product of human greed ('lusts in the soul'). Simplicity is counted alongside peace, integrity, community and equality in the inter-related list of Quaker testimonies.

If you visit a Quaker Meeting you'll find at least someone engaged in peace work; maybe peace education, conflict-resolution, nonviolent activism or humanitarian relief. On occasion you'll meet someone who has followed different peace-leadings perhaps as an army chaplain or an advisor to a peacekeeping force. If you were to meet Nozizwe Madlala-Routledge you would be talking with a (now former) Deputy Minister of Defence.

How can it be then that one of the world's historic peace churches can also contain such variety of pathways to peace? In response, Quakers often tell a story which has attained the status of fable. It concerns William Penn who is best known as founder of the US state of Pennsylvania (also often supposed to be the model for the man on the Quaker Oats packets, which – let me clarify here – has no connection at all to the Society of Friends). Penn became a convinced Quaker in his youth, but still carried a sword, as was then the custom for men of his background. He asked George Fox whether he should continue to do so, and received the reply 'I advise thee to wear it as long as thou canst.' When they next met, Penn was no longer armed. When Fox asked where his sword was, Penn replied 'I have taken thy advice; I wore it as long as I could.' The ongoing popularity of the story sheds light more clearly on the Quaker approach to peace; to each seek inward peace in the company of a Quaker Meeting or private contemplation, and to listen for the guidance of the inner light.[8]

This does not imply a rejection of conflict. Indeed, another early manifestation of the Peace Testimony was a project called *The Lamb's War*. A book of the same name by James Naylor gave articulation to the movement's practice of encouraging people to turn away from the words of those church ministers who endorsed war and injustice and instead to listen to the inner light – the Light of Christ, the Lamb, which would lead people away from violent acts towards action for peace. Although this led to severe repression, including large numbers of Quakers being beaten, jailed and in some cases killed, the persecution appeared only to add to the movement's strength, resolve and numbers.

The Lamb's War could be seen as an anticipation of modern day nonviolent civil disobedience, echoed in the twentieth century, for example, by English suffragette Sylvia Pankhurst who proclaimed that 'the true pacifist is a rebel against the present organisation of society, and only as we...despise the gain of privilege and oppression shall our feet be guided in the way of peace.' So too it can be heard in the words of Martin Luther King who in his *Letter from a Birmingham Jail*, called out for criticism 'the white moderate who is more devoted to order than to justice, who prefers a negative peace which is the absence of tension to a positive peace which is the presence of justice'.[9]

King's friend and advisor Bayard Rustin helped popularise the phrase 'speak truth to power'. In another memorable quotation he eloquently captures how pacifism is the very opposite of passivity, declaring: 'We need in every community a group of angelic troublemakers. Our power is in our ability to make things unworkable. The only weapon we have is our bodies and we need to tuck them in places so the wheels won't turn.'[10]

Conflict happens as soon as two or more people have different interests. Practitioners of peace frequently say that conflict is essential for human progress and for confronting injustice. The challenge of peacemaking is to do it in a way that respects human life.[11]

But perhaps it is easier said than done. Are there circumstances in which an opponent is so evil that war itself is needed to bring about peace?

Chapter 2

War is the greater evil

Almost everyone old enough to remember knows where they were on 11 September 2001. The smoking buildings. People running and screaming. Bodies falling from height. Fireballs in the streets. Over and over again, the images of planes flying into the twin towers of the World Trade Center in New York were replayed on television. In all nearly 3000 people died, broadcast into people's living rooms across the world.

Before the day was out, US President George W. Bush gave an address in which he used the word 'evil' four times. Then UK Prime Minister Tony Blair took to the airwaves, promising not to rest 'until this evil is driven from our world'. A 'War on Terror' was declared, and nine days later the US began bombing Afghanistan with UK support. Despite it having no connection to the 9/11 attacks, Bush then sought to extend the war to other countries which he termed an 'axis of evil', including Iraq. So rarely far from the headlines, the question of evil seemed difficult to avoid.

The language of evil isn't much used by Quakers —at least not within the liberal tradition of which I am part. Ask a Quaker what they believe and the chances are they'll say something about working for peace and something about that of God residing in all (that of good for more secular Friends). The two statements are connected. If all people have within them a divine spark, then by extension we are all equal and it doesn't make sense for some people to claim justification for killing others.

What about the idea that we each have evil within us as well? A Quaker might answer that evil is not so much a force as an absence, or lack of openness to the Light. Another might reply that even if we do each have evil within us, then it still makes no sense to suppress it through killing, which then really would lead to a war of all against all.

Perhaps surprisingly, given the aversion to the language of evil, the word is used 44 times in the spiritual anthology *Quaker Faith and Practice,* which reflects and shapes the lives of Quakers in Britain. Within it contributors name inequality, involuntary unemployment, homelessness, torture, slavery, fascism and war as societal evils perhaps at their most dangerous when they are so deep rooted that they can become, 'accepted, even by the best minds, as part of the providential ordering of life'.[12]

The idea of war itself as an evil is difficult to square with the characterisation so often presented by politicians – of evil existing only on the other side of a conflict, capable of possessing people to the extent that that it can only be suppressed through organised violence.

Calculating the cost

There are some who offer a more nuanced view, justifying war in some instances as the 'lesser of two evils', as was argued at the outset of the wars in Afghanistan and Iraq. This approach invites people to assess which evil outweighs the other, but exactly how to do this remains unclear. To stay with the case of the 'War on Terror'; there was no official body count in Afghanistan, but even the lower estimates suggest that the invasion caused the death of 3000 people in the first few years, rising to tens of thousands in the years that followed. A survey counting only reported deaths emerging from the Iraq War names a figure of 268,000 – at least 17,000 of whom were killed directly by US-led forces. At the upper end, it has been suggested that the figure could be more than a million.[13]

Measuring casualties is difficult enough. But there is yet more to consider. Should our assessment of the lesser evil be weighted for civilians as opposed to combatants? Does this change if the army on one or both sides is conscripted? How do we count the injured, the psychologically scarred, the grieving families or the unfunded social projects as money is diverted to war? Do we do it by the type of torture incurred; somehow measuring one side's human rights abuses against the other? Should we compare the potential number of deaths on each side had an intervention not occurred? How can we know how many are not yet dead but will be due to cycles of violence set in train? Is it possible to account for the impact of war on the environment or on animals? Can we measure the effects on the population at home, as people are taught through their government's action that it's OK to kill people from other countries?

Even to begin to construe such a formula reveals the impossibility of calculating such an unknowable sum. Even if we could it would rest on the assumption that an armed intervention would achieve the desired result. As we know from experience that can never be known for sure. To the extent that there is a calculation in Western countries, it is likely that the lives of working class people and people of colour – both at home and in those places that are attacked – are valued by decision makers as less important than the children of their own country's elites.

The flipside is the 'greater-of-two-evils' argument, widely used in the case against torture and the death penalty, as innocent people can accidentally be harmed and because the practices are ineffective at achieving their stated goals. The invasion of Iraq is also sometimes characterised as on balance the greater of two evils. It emerged in the aftermath that whilst Iraq did not possess weapons capable of mass destruction the invasion did cause tens of thousands of deaths and gave new life to terrorist networks. For the pacifist, killing is always wrong, so to add to it adds to the wrong done overall.

Perhaps the argument has been most eloquently made by the novelist Leo Tolstoy who wrote in his essay 'What I Believe' that:

During thousands and thousands of years you have tried to

annihilate evil by evil, and you have not annihilated it; you have but increased it... Even their cleverest, most learned men close their eyes to the simple, self-evident truth that if we admit the right of one man to resist what he considers as evil by violence, we cannot refuse another the right to resist by violence what he in his turn may consider as evil.[14]

Taking a longer view, one study estimates that the US Government alone has been responsible for the deaths of 20 million people in 37 different countries since 1945.[15] Would the argument that violence can suppress evil justify an attack on the United States? For some of its enemies, it does. But not for those elites ordering bombing attacks on other countries. Nor for those peacemakers that are trying to remove the causes of war.

There is a difference between non-resistance to evil and nonviolent resistance to evil. The former stands back while the latter consistently gets involved in long-term nonviolent action for peace and for justice. So it is that over centuries Quakers, amongst others, have been part of nonviolent campaigns against slavery, poverty, capital punishment, the arms trade, nuclear weapons, climate change, homophobia, sexism and racism – all of which play their parts in war and the preparations for war and all of which are inherently violent in themselves.

But is a pacifist stance a targeted accusation against soldiers? Quite the opposite; it is an accusation against society as currently arranged. As Tolstoy put it, extreme acts of violence happen because they are 'divided among a number that none shall bear the sole responsibility, or recognize how unnatural all cruelty is. Some make laws, others apply them; others, again, drill their fellow-creatures into habits of discipline...who in their turn, do violence to others'.[16] Like Tolstoy himself, serving and former soldiers are, and have often been, amongst the most eloquent and effective advocates for peace, having seen the effects of – and been ordered to enact – their governments' brutal decisions.

Yet this can be a hard thing to recognise. Humans naturally find it difficult to acknowledge our participation in vast systems of violent injustice. To prevent ourselves from being overwhelmed by the inherent complexities of the world we create dichotomies between 'good' and 'evil'. This has perhaps no more been the case than through the language of religion, and Christianity in particular, which deserves to be looked at in greater depth.

Chapter 3

Thou shalt not kill

Christianity does not have a good record when it comes to war. The Crusades of the eleventh, twelfth and thirteenth centuries still rank amongst the most hypocritical acts of religious violence in history, as the church called upon Europeans to wage 'holy wars' in the Middle East with effects still felt today. Though different words were used, they set a pattern: When Spanish and Portuguese *conquistadores* massacred the people, claimed the lands and stole the resources of what we now call Latin America they did so with the active participation of the church. In the course of the colonisation of North America too, religious authorities were complicit in the genocide of millions of Native Americans.

But still it continued. In the nineteenth century, Europe's brutal colonisation of Africa took place under the guise of a concern for ongoing slavery, proposing 'commerce, civilisation and Christianity' as a solution and an excuse to lay claim to the majority of land on the continent. When most of the land was taken, conquest turned to competition between European powers, spilling into open war with one-another in 1914. Again, churches on all sides helped mobilise support for their respective governments' actions, each believing their countries to be engaged in justified wars of self-defence. What was called at the time the 'Great War' or the 'War to End All Wars' is now damningly referred to as World War One.

Such is the record of institutional Christianity that accusations of encouraging violence are at the fore of the critique of organised religion. People offering that critique might be surprised to discover that based on what we know of his short worldly life, Jesus may well have agreed.

A preacher of peace

Jesus' first public words that we know of are found in the four-page lecture we nowadays call the 'Sermon on the Mount'. It is introduced with a series of blessings including of 'the peacemakers, for they will be called children of God'. The sermon that follows is utterly unambiguous and the message is reaffirmed several times over. Jesus begins with an exploration of the Hebrew commandment *thou shalt not kill*. This he endorses and emphasises by encouraging forgiveness and reconciliation in the face of disputes of all kinds. He then moves on to the ancient teaching 'an eye for an eye and a tooth for a tooth' which he negates directly: 'if anyone strikes you on the right cheek, turn to him the other also'.[17]

Not willing to let the point be misunderstood Jesus continues; 'you have heard that it was said "love your neighbour and hate your enemy". But I tell you love your enemy and pray for those that persecute you' and goes still further: 'How can you say to your brother "let me take the speck out of your eye" when there is the log in your own eye. You hypocrite! First take out the log from your own eye and then you will see clearly to take the speck out of your brother's eye.' The sermon ends in poetic flourish to make certain to all that he means what he says: 'Everyone who hears these words of mine and acts on them is like a wise man who built his house on the rock...But everyone who hears these words of mine and does not act on them is like a foolish man who built his house on sand.'

There is no report of Jesus ever inflicting violence on another person in any of the four accounts of his life which made it into the Bible. There is certainly conflict: Jesus is arrested following a confrontation at the temple where he and his disciples disrupt the activity there, driving the sheep and cattle away with a hastily made whip. But there is no account of any people being physically harmed and certainly not killed. At the time of his arrest Jesus' friends have the opportunity to defend him with weapons, but instead he instructs Peter– leader of the movement after his death – to put away his sword.

Just as Jesus' revolutionary outlook may come as a surprise to onlookers today, I imagine that he was a surprise to people of his time as well. The prophecies of a Messiah invited the image of a military man who would liberate his people from oppression. Instead they got an unarmed preacher of peace, who taught people how to win change without violence.

One of the first recorded groups to collectively renounce war and reject its institutions was the early Christian church. As with the church of modern times, there was a diversity of interpretation within it, but nevertheless many of the most prominent early Christian writers taught nonviolence and peace. Ignatius of Antioch, for example, called for the abolition of warfare and Origen declared that, 'We Christians do not become fellow soldiers with the Emperor, even if he presses for this.' Tertullian openly spoke of converting soldiers to Christianity so that they would refuse to fight. The earliest conscientious objector that we know of was a Christian.[18]

So how was it that the understanding of Christianity would change so much? Most historians trace it to the year 312 when the Roman Emperor Constantine carried a Christian symbol into a battle which he went on to win. It began a process in which Christianity would become the official religion of the empire. Although a steady stream of smaller, non-conformist Christian groups carried the torch of peace in the centuries that followed, on the whole the church became something new: a faith that would take sides to help one group of people wage organised violence against another.

Just War Theory

Seeking to reconcile the peaceful inheritance of Jesus and the violence of the wars of the state, the fifth-century theologian Augustine of Hippo, coined a new phrase, 'just war'. Updated into 'Just War Theory' by Thomas Aquinas in the thirteenth century and supplemented by later writers, it forms a more-or-less coherent set of criteria to assess the conditions under which it could be considered justified to go to war and for how a just war should be fought.

Even in an increasingly secular society, the theory is still widely referred to today. As recently as 2015 when the UK Houses of Parliament voted to launch airstrikes in Syria, the Archbishop of Canterbury gave a speech in the House of Lords declaring his view that the just war criteria had been met, although the government must be aware of 'doing the right thing in such a wrong way that it becomes the wrong thing'.[19]

In its summarised form, the conditions for a just war are usually presented in six points:

1 The war must be for a just cause (this might include self-defence, defending other nations from aggression or preventing an attack)
2 The war must be lawfully declared by a legitimate authority such as the state
3 The intention behind the war must be good and not merely in the interests of the country's rulers (this would rule out war for resources, commercial interests or because of personal machismo)
4 All other ways of resolving the problem should have been tried first
5 There must be a reasonable chance of success
6 The means used must be in proportion to the end that the war seeks to achieve.

A second set of criteria were added later which instruct how a just war should be fought:

1 Innocent people and non-combatants should not be

harmed
2 Only appropriate force should be used
3 Internationally agreed conventions regulating war must be obeyed.

No study I can find has yet attempted to work out how many of the 1763 wars recorded in the Encyclopaedia of Wars has in practice succeeded in meeting all of these broad parameters for a just war. Suffice to say, not many do: The provision on just cause would rule out the various wars for land, gold and oil, including all of the wars of conquest and colonialism. The provision on war as the last resort would rule out all wars by governments that have not been actively engaged over time in efforts to promote peace and justice. Perhaps most powerfully, the provision against harming civilians would rule out almost all of the wars of the past three centuries, during which the proportion of civilian deaths in war has averaged 50%. According to Graça Machel in her role as the UN Secretary General's Expert on the Impact of Armed Conflict on Children, by the end of the twentieth century, war was killing and maiming more children than soldiers.[20] In recent years it has become increasingly common for attackers to promise to use advanced technology enabling only 'precision' bombing which takes all feasible precautions to avoid civilian casualties. The 2017 war against the ISIS-held city of Raqqa in Syria was initially boasted of as the most 'precise air campaign in the history of armed conflict'. But following the attacks, UN war crimes investigators uncovered a 'staggering loss of civilian life' as a result of the bombing. Rights groups showed that the casualties included children, victims of ISIS and people attempting to escape the city. The artillery shells dropped had a margin of error of more than 100 metres. The chemical white phosphorous was also used as a weapon by US forces.[21] In the aftermath, military leaders conceded that war cannot happen without taking civilians' lives.

Modern technology should also prompt a rethink of what we mean by self-defence. Once the words conjured the idea of lining up foot-soldiers near a country's border in order to prevent a rival army's advance, but modern wars are fought differently. In the age of the drone, nuclear weapons and cyber-warfare, Governments now have the ability to inflict mass murder through the pressing of buttons on computers from thousands of miles away. Counter-intuitive as it may seem, the best way to defend populations is to work for mutual disarmament and the nonviolent resolution of conflict.

The seemingly straightforward question of wars for defence is made more difficult by the pattern of politicians explaining the case untruthfully. The 2003 war in Iraq was explained as one of 'pre-emptive self-defence' based on what turned out to be false claims that Iraq possessed weapons of mass destruction. The USA's escalation of the war in Vietnam was justified as an act of self-defence following what turned out to be an untrue claim that the US warship Maddox had sustained an unprovoked attack in international waters whilst on routine patrol.[22]

This has extended in to war in the name of defending others. This too needs to be approached with care, as the language of just cause often disguises other motives. Part of the propaganda case for the USA's involvement in the first Gulf War involved what turned out to be false testimony by a woman who claimed she had seen Iraqi soldiers remove babies from incubators and leave them to die. She was later revealed to be the Kuwaiti ambassador's daughter acting as part of a PR campaign. The deceit was revealed only after the war.[23]

The most powerful case against the just war approach though is also the most obvious: A just war that implies God's blessing necessitates that a just war as seen from one side could not by the same method be understood as a just war by the other. The fact that in practice faith leaders have long used the theory to declare the justice only for their own country's side of international conflicts reveals that the theory is not fit for purpose. Nevertheless worldwide, the funds invested in building peace are a fraction of those spent preparing for war.

Rather than turn to others to dictate our morality then, the Quaker turns to the light within and asks what *would* Jesus do? Would Jesus sell weapons, torture people, develop the means of robotic warfare or press the nuclear button? Or would Jesus put those resources into projects that build peace, reconciliation, understanding and justice? The question has long been asked, as the anti-war activist and future MP Alfred Salter did in the shadow of World War One. The answer he received was clear:

What would Christ do in my place? Would Christ fight... Look Christ out in France thrusting his bayonet into the body of a German workman. See! The Son of God with a machine gun ambushing a column of German infantry, catching them unaware in a lane and mowing them down in their helplessness...

No! No! That picture is an impossible one, *and we all know it.*[24]

Chapter 4

The power of nonviolence

Sooner or later (and probably sooner) every pacifist will be asked the question of what should be done about governments that commit violent acts?

The first answer is of course 'I wouldn't support them in the first place'. From Mobutu Sese-Seko in Zaire to Saddam Hussein in Iraq, many of the world's most brutal dictators of recent decades were assisted to power through Western intervention and a great deal more have directly or indirectly benefitted from weapons made or sold in countries that lay claim to a belief in promoting democracy.

After such a history, the assertion that only external bombing or invasions can bring democracy is both disingenuous and demonstrably false. Nevertheless, the question remains: What are the alternatives to violence in transitioning from dictatorship to democracy? And, indeed, what are the alternatives to violence in challenging those governments that call themselves democratic, but that nevertheless engage in violent abuse? The question is all the more engaging because it is being answered in different ways all around the world, through the means of nonviolent struggle.

In a 2011 study charting the success and failure of over 300 anti-regime, anti-occupation or independence campaigns over 106 years, the security scholars Erica Chenoweth and Maria Stephan found that unarmed-people power campaigns have proven more than twice as likely to win full or partial success compared to those using armed resistance. This remained the case regardless of the type of regime and allowing for a range of levels of repression.[25]

Probably the most comprehensive study of *why* nonviolent

action works has been offered by Gene Sharp – a Boston academic who published tens of books between 1973 and his death in 2018. Each one demonstrates how authoritarian systems can be dismantled without resorting to war. Beginning with the simple recognition that the power of elites is derived from the co-operation of the ruled, he constructed a system to help movements identify which 'pillars' a regime relies on most for its power. Perhaps it is the military, taxes, international support, ideological influence or control of the workforce. By identifying a ruler's sources of power we're equipped to make a strategy which erodes those pillars one by one. He argued that every regime has an *Achilles Heel*, in which the ruling elites are weak and in which the movement is strong. It is very rare that the weak point of an authoritarian regime is violence.[26]

Although similar ideas can be found as far back in history as the time of the Roman Republic, perhaps the first person to both develop a theory and test it at scale was a lawyer from India who was a spiritual thinker and a shrewd political strategist.

The emergence of People Power

Concerned for the rights of Indians in South Africa, a young lawyer called Mohandas Gandhi made it his mission to learn about freedom struggles around the world. He studied the suffragettes of England, boycotts in China, revolutionary upheavals in Russia and the ideas of Henry Thoreau in the United States who had written his essay *On the Duty of Civil Disobedience* following his imprisonment for resisting the US/Mexico war.[27]

Reading in the light of his Hindu faith and culture, Gandhi developed the moral and strategic framework he called *Satyagraha* – which roughly translates as 'truth force', or 'soul force'. Through a programme of nonviolent strikes, boycotts, marches and non-cooperation, he became known as the most prominent leader of the movements that first won greater liberties for Indians in South Africa and went on to win independence for India.

A theology student named Martin Luther King discovered Gandhi's work whilst enrolled in a Pennsylvania seminary. Reflecting later he wrote: 'Prior to reading Gandhi I had concluded that the ethics of Jesus were only effective in individual relationships...When racial groups and nations were in conflict a more realistic approach seemed necessary. But after reading Gandhi I saw how utterly mistaken I was.'[28] Five years later, King rose to prominence as an eloquent spokesperson for the Montgomery Bus Boycott begun by fellow activist Rosa Parks, and then for the Civil Rights Movement more broadly.

In a recent interview, civil rights leader Diane Nash called Gandhi's way of making change without killing fellow human beings 'the most important invention of the twentieth century'.[29] After attending training in nonviolent action with James Lawson (a student of Gandhi) Nash became a pioneer of the sit-in movement that led to the first successful desegregation of lunch counters in the US. As chair of the Student Nonviolent Coordinating Committee (SNCC) she co-organised the Freedom Rides which helped desegregate interstate travel, mobilised for the mass civil rights march which preceded the new civil rights legislation, and then, alongside others, co-led the Selma campaign which won a new Voting Rights Act.[30]

The ideas kept on spreading, though the words in each context changed. In Ghana, Gandhi's example influenced the largely nonviolent campaign to become the first country in Sub-Saharan Africa to win independence from British rule, where the approach was dubbed 'Positive Action' by independence leader Kwame Nkrumah. Although not a pacifist on principle, Nkrumah's pragmatic nonviolent programme helped his successful election as Prime Minister even whilst incarcerated in prison. From that point on, independence was unstoppable and was won in 1957.

The ideas came to the peace movement of Britain through the writing of Richard B. Gregg, a Quaker and colleague of Gandhi.

His book *The Power of Nonviolence* was studied by Peace Pledge Union groups across the country and inspired experimentation with nonviolent tactics new to the movement such as sit-down protests. It then influenced the decision to form the Direct Action Committee against nuclear war, for whom what we know as the 'peace sign' was designed and first used on a march to the Aldermaston Atomic Weapons Research Establishment in 1958.[31]

In the 1960s the ideas gained a hearing in the United States Migrants Rights Movement. Campaign leader Dolores Huerta later explained 'I must have read that book on Gandhi three times, because it had so many lessons for me, and ways that I could cope with the racism I was living with.'[32] After meeting fellow organiser Cesar Chavez, they began talking about how they could organise a trade union based on Gandhi's philosophy. The result was the United Farm Workers, who led a nationwide boycott which resulted in the entire California table grape industry agreeing to collective bargaining with the union.

Meanwhile in Canada it was around the kitchen table of Quaker couple Dorothy and Irving Stowe that a plan was made to stop nuclear testing in Alaska, again inspired by Gandhi's thinking. The people gathered there resolved to sail a boat into the test zone in 1971. The boat never made it, but the public furore led to the test being cancelled the following year. The name of that boat, Greenpeace, became the name of the best-known environmental organisation in the world.

It was in 1986 that the broad approach of mass nonviolent civil resistance gained the name we still use today: 'People Power'. Faced with a brutal dictatorship in the Philippines, nonviolence training equipped 500,000 people to nonviolently defend ballot-boxes in a tense election. Theirs was the first to be called a People Power revolution.

Why Civil Resistance Works

Gene Sharp noted that many successful nonviolent campaigners have not been ideologically or spiritually pacifist but instead are people simply looking for the most effective route to change. In his view, the best route to stopping war was not to protest against it, but instead to create a realistic alternative.

One of the principal promoters of Sharp's work was not a pacifist either, but a retired army general, who introduced Sharp's theories to the pro-democracy youth movement *Otpor!* in Serbia. *Otpor!* went on to play a decisive part in bringing down the murderous regime that oppressed them. From there the ideas spread to other Eastern European countries challenging authoritarian governments. At least some of the revolutionaries who co-led Egypt's 2011 unarmed uprising had received training in strategic nonviolence from colleagues in Serbia.[33]

Nonviolent struggles have been waged against governments ruling in the name of both left and right and have likewise involved movements with left, right and centrist leanings. Some have achieved their goals, others haven't. In every situation though, the choice of strategic nonviolence over armed conflict has saved countless lives that could have otherwise been lost.

It may be that part of the reason for the success of nonviolent struggle is the scale of participation that is possible including many people from different walks of life. People who work for armies or security services are more likely to disobey orders to fire at demonstrators if it is likely that their friends or family members are in the crowds. Greater numbers also broaden the menu of tactical options as movements can swap between concentrated mass actions like demonstrations and dispersed mass actions like strikes. According to Chenoweth and Stephan's calculation, it takes only an average of 3.5% of a population engaged in strategic nonviolent conflict, to make a regime fall.[34] Supporting 3.5% of a population to participate in a nonviolent movement is no small feat – but nor is it by any means impossible.

In contrast, armed uprisings tend to be smaller and rely much more on support from outside their country. When 'successful', armed uprisings often lead to the authoritarian logic of the military being transferred into government, which results in the ongoing suppression of dissent. With violent means of change legitimised by the government's own path to power, opposition then becomes more likely to be violent too, leading to an ongoing cycle of violence.

Does nonviolent action always work?

It is important to be cautious with even the best-researched statistics. Citing the best-known pacifist case-studies of the past century, some critics of nonviolence point out that both the Indian independence campaign and the US Civil Rights Movement had significant armed components. The argument is compounded by the case that the independence movement in India may have won self-government but left many of the economic dynamics of colonialism in place. So too the Civil Rights Movement by no means defeated racism.

For many social justice activists, revolution is a participatory, on-going process, rather a period in history. Maintaining and advancing the victories of freedom movements needs ongoing pressure. To the extent that the use of nonviolent strategy did not result in everything the movement worked for, violent tactics did not achieve those objectives either.

By way of contrast, advocates of armed struggle often cite the twentieth-century revolutions in Russia, China, Cuba, Algeria and Vietnam as examples of change achieved through military means. Here the argument works the other way: There were significant examples of nonviolent civil resistance in many of those cases – Cuba and Russia in particular. We have no way of testing what would have happened if nonviolent action had been the predominant strategy. We do know, however, that, whatever the justice or otherwise of the cause, where organised violence is the dominant approach of the revolutionary movement, the violence tends to continue in the government's treatment of citizens after the transition. It is not a matter of the means justifying the ends. The means shape the ends.

Chenoweth and Stephan have their critics amongst peacemakers too. Reviewing *Why Civil Resistance Works* for *Peace News*, former Direct Action Committee chair Michael Randle reflects wistfully that,

> whilst civil resistance campaigns have played a central role in delivering both transitions to democracy and the removal of extreme injustices within constitutional democracies, the method has been less effective in bringing to power governments prepared to renounce lethal violence abroad. For example, the former Communist countries of Eastern Europe have not disarmed and instead have for the most part joined the NATO military alliance.[35]

We might add to this the mixed success of the peace movements of Western Europe and North America. Although public pressure has been part of the reason why more nuclear weapons haven't been fired, no approach of any type has yet won global nuclear disarmament. So too in the environmental movement, nonviolent action has proved effective at stymieing dirty infrastructure projects, but the movement has yet to win at a scale that would halt global climate change.

Important as it is, mere protest is not enough. To win big it must be joined to a structural critique which addresses violence throughout society. Such a view has been termed an *anti-militarist* approach. If we seek to unpick those oppressions and act as part of a wider movement for collective liberation, we could call it an *intersectional* approach.[36]Without such a commitment, nonviolent action is incomplete and will be incapable of abolishing war. Every pacifist should remember that part of waging nonviolence is the struggle for equality including in the movement itself.

Chapter 5

Gender, sexuality and peace

'Wars are not isolated phenomena. There are ways of leading up to them and away from them, behaviour which provokes them and which calms them and stops them. They are part of the human process of relationships on an individual, a national and an international scale.' So explained the Quaker Women's Group in a lecture in 1986.[37]

One in three women and girls experience sexual violence at some point in their life.[38] The vast majority of terrorist attacks are by men, who often have histories of domestic violence.[39] At the time of writing, 1 in 5 UK LGBT+ people have experienced a hate crime because of their sexuality or gender identity in the last year alone.[40] From the earliest times to the present day, rape has been used as a weapon of war. These facts are not unconnected. Macho ideas that connect sex (especially heterosexual sex) with violence are woven into our societies and built in to our languages. They begin even before we are conceived.

If someone 'hits on someone' it means they want to have sex with them. If people are 'banging', 'smashing' or 'nailing', they're having sex. If someone gets pregnant they might be described as 'knocked up'. If a man is 'firing blanks' it means he is infertile. It isn't uncommon for a man to refer to an ex-partner as a 'conquest'.

If you have a child who is a boy, the chances are that someone will give him a toy soldier or a gun to play with. It's unlikely he will get through his teens without playing a violent video-game, hearing an 'Armed Forces Day' speaker, going to an air-show or watching an action film. Any of these may form part of an army recruitment strategy. Many of them perpetuate the myth that men must fight as part of their manhood. In the schoolyard, the street and the nightclub, conflicts are catalysed by macho notions of 'saving face' in a culture where power exerted through violence is a mark of male status and self-image. If your boy tries to act differently he may well be called 'girl' or 'faggot'. If so he is being taught through our culture that hetero-normative masculinity and violence go together.

This is reflected institutionally. Many of the world's national armies permit only non-trans heterosexual men to enrol in combat roles. Those that have become more inclusive in their admissions have done so typically under the twin pressures of internal recruitment crises and external campaigns. Always there has been opposition to such reforms, often from the very top. Despite public relations campaigns seeking to clean up the army's image, frequent reports emerge of homophobic prejudice. In the US army 2 in 5 women endure sexual trauma during service.[41]

In the light of such a situation, the crisis of violence needs to be understood as at least in part a crisis caused by the prevalence of patriarchy and the problems of toxic masculinity. Pervasive as it is, trying to understand and unpick this is part of the role of the pacifist too.

Feminism and anti-militarism

From the earliest days of the feminist movement, war has been part of the critique of male dominance. Offering what we'd now call an anti-militarist critique, Mary Wollstonecraft wrote in A Vindication of the Rights of Woman (1792) of the systems of hierarchy and rank in a standing army as antithetical to freedom more broadly. The first written publication calling for votes for women was produced in 1847 by a feminist, abolitionist and Quaker, Anne Knight. In it she argued that the nations of the earth would never be well governed until women were fully represented. Many who campaigned for the cause of votes for women in the decades that followed did so with a vision that equal rights would be a step towards a world without war.[42]

In 1915 women from countries across the world braved restrictions to travel to The Hague and attempted to organise internationally against the 'Great War', forming the grouping that became the Women's International League for Peace and Freedom. Not everyone agreed though. On the outbreak of war, a great split had emerged in the UK women's movement, when suffragette leaders Emmeline and Christabel Pankhurst put their campaign for the vote on hold and turned their efforts instead towards recruiting men for the army and women for the munitions factories. They also encouraged young women to give white feathers to men of military age who were not fighting as an accusatory symbol of cowardice.

This 'feminised militarism' grew from the idea that the war was at least in part a battle to protect British women from the violence of men of other countries. Virginia Woolf wanted no part in such arguments. In her pacifist polemic *Three Guineas,* she accuses her own country of exploiting her gender, denying her an education and refusing any share in its possessions, declaring: 'If you insist on fighting to protect me or "our country", let it be understood, soberly and rationally that you are fighting to gratify a sex-instinct which I cannot share, to procure benefits I have not shared and probably will not share...In fact, as a woman I have no country. As a woman I want no country. As a woman my country is the whole world.'[43]

Yet despite the shared journey of feminist and nonviolent thought, ostensibly nonviolent movements have been marred by misogyny. To return to the example of Indian independence: Gandhi's farsightedness regarding the possibilities of nonviolent struggle was not matched by an appreciation of gender equality. It is likely that the non-inclusive means influenced the outcome. India's liberation from Britain was not accompanied by Indian women's liberation from patriarchy.

So too in the US Civil Rights Movement, behind-the-scenes

organiser Ella Baker expressed her concern that most of the work was done by women and most of the decisions were made by men, in replication of wider church structures. Septima Clark – often referred to as the 'Mother of the Civil Rights Movement' – had some even more direct words for her male colleagues: 'Those men didn't have any faith in women, none whatsoever. They just thought that women were sex symbols and had no contributions to make.'[44]

Calling out the inequality in the movement, civil rights activists Mary King and Casey Hayden wrote an article observing that women 'seem to be caught up in a common-law caste system that operates, sometimes subtly, forcing them to work around or outside hierarchical structures of power which may exclude them. Women seem to be placed in the same position of assumed subordination in personal situations too. It is a caste system which, at its worst, uses and exploits women'.[45] The document became a foundational text in the formation of the Women's Liberation Movement.

The second-wave feminist movement of the 1960s immediately faced homophobic attacks in the media, as defenders of male dominance sought to undermine movements for justice by encouraging revulsion at the sexuality of some of the movement's leaders. This experience represented a strong continuation from previous struggles.

The feminist movement, peace movement and movement against homophobia converged again in the 1980s in the form of an all-women camp protesting cruise missiles at Greenham Common in England. The campaign was initiated by 36 women who walked from South Wales to deliver a letter. When their request for a meeting was refused, they decided to stay. Others came to join them and on days of action they reached 30,000 people in number, holding hands around the base. Echoing the experience of movements past they were attacked as 'leftie lesbians'. The protesters were of different sexualities, but it exposed a larger issue. As the writer of a lesbian and gay history of the 1980s points out: 'in the bizarre logic of the pro-nuclear lobby, having the ability to inflict Armageddon on millions of innocent people was far better than the ability to love another person of the same sex.'[46]

Piecing it together

One of the documents inspired by Greenham Common was the group-written *Piecing it Together,* which began from the standpoint that 'nothing that happens in our personal lives is without a meaning in public life...in other words, the personal is political.' [47] Although it was written more than quarter of a century ago, the document is worth pausing on, as it shines a light on live discussions in the peace movement, which – then and now–pose questions for pacifists.

There are some who simultaneously oppose abortion at home while supporting foreign policies that lead to the deaths of children abroad. Many pacifists understandably point out this hypocrisy, which for some is based in the idea that all killing including abortion is wrong. Whilst acknowledging this position, the writers of *Piecing it Together* see it in wider context:

> We also look to the violence done to the woman who is made to have a child against her will, including, often, conception against her will. We look at the question in the context of male sexual domination, of death by backstreet abortionists, at the deaths of thousands of women...and there can be no doubt that we demand the woman's right to choose.

There is also the question of self-defence in the context of a sexual attack. The authors write:

> An individual woman facing a violent man still confronts the problem of what she as an individual will do (take it, fight

back, and leave) but her choice is made easier if she knows that other women share her experience that she is visible and what is happening is wrong. As long as individual women at home or on the streets face violence without a very active support to stop that violence, we assert the right to defend ourselves from that victimisation, including physically if necessary. The basis of most women's self-defence is precisely defence – not hurting, maiming, degrading or killing our attackers but talking, shouting, running and only if necessary hitting.

The writers also take issue with the idea that women are natural peacemakers, arguing:

Whilst there is no doubt that the qualities of caring and nurturance that most women learn from our infancy are crucial to the development of the human community, we should be insisting that men learn precisely these qualities...appealing to women as 'Mothers' relieves men of the responsibility for becoming carers and nurturers whilst belittling women who aren't biological mothers, either by choice or by necessity.

In recent decades a school of feminist international relations has emerged from the peace movement, painting war itself as a manifestation of patriarchy, with nuclear weapons representing giant phalluses pointing at one another, echoing the Greenham slogan 'take the toys from the boys'. So too, colonialism cannot be seen simply as a process of one country dominating others, but as a power structure through which men in some countries exoticise and commit sexual violence against women in others. The eco-feminist perspective, which was so named around the same time, extends this argument to the violence against Mother Earth.

For some people the one exception to the wrongfulness of deploying armed forces is the example of United Nations' peacekeeping operations. They are made up of armies from around the world and invited to keep warring parties apart. What they don't do is provide an alternative to militarism, demonstrated by the multiple sexual abuse scandals they have faced. While gender inequality, toxic masculinity and pervasive militarism continue to shape our societies, even well-intentioned interventions can have the effect of entrenching structural violence.

In her bestselling 2017 book *Why I'm No Longer Talking to White People about Race* Reni Eddo-Lodge writes:

Feminism at its best is a movement that works to liberate all people who have been economically, socially, and culturally marginalised by an ideological system that has been designed for them to fail. That means disabled people, black people, trans people, women and non-binary people, LGB people and working-class people. The idea of campaigning for equality has to be complicated if we are to untangle the mess that we are in.[48]

The peace movement needs to be similarly complicated.

Chapter 6

Pacifism and anti-racism

It isn't enough for pacifism to be feminist and in solidarity with LGBT+ people. It needs to be anti-racist too. War relies on the idea that some people's lives are worth more than others. When this valuation is based on skin colour, ethnicity or place of birth it is a racist idea which has led to some of the most brutal acts of violence in history.

From the fifteenth century onwards, untold millions of people were forcibly removed from Africa as slaves. In Britain and the US the practice was outlawed in the nineteenth century. But as the academic and activist Angela Davis asks, 'what about the whole scaffolding of racist ideology that was necessary to keep an entire people enslaved. Was that abolished?'.[49]

To be a pacifist in the spirit of *Salaam/Shalom* involves personal reflection on the seeds of war, and the extent to which they are able to grow because of racial inequality. Such inequality can manifest throughout society, including in movements for peace. This need not lead to paralysis so much as to the exact opposite; there are points of intervention every day where oppression and capacity for violence is being built which can instead be transformed into moments to progress towards peace. It also means acting with movements for racial justice as vigorously as working against wars.

Quakers in movements for racial justice

Advocates for peace – including many Quakers – played a role in the movement against slavery especially in Britain and North America. Friends – amongst them the abolitionists Lucretia Mott and John Woolman – boycotted products of slavery and set up 'Free Produce Groceries' to support others to do so. Influenced by Woolman, Levi Coffin was a founder of what became known as the 'Underground Railroad' supporting enslaved people to escape to freedom. In both countries Quakers co-founded and co-financed influential campaigning organisations that persistently petitioned politicians against the institution of slavery. The prominence of Quakers in anti-slavery histories means that Friends have a name as allies for racial justice. But today and in history, racial inequality within the Society of Friends must be acknowledged in order to address it. This begins by being honest about the past. Although the Society of Friends was the first institution to disown members for 'owning' enslaved people, nearly a century passed between the earliest Quakers speaking out against slavery and the corporate decision to make not being an enslaver a condition of membership. Indeed, it was in part for his anti-slavery activism that the 'first revolutionary abolitionist' Benjamin Lay was himself disowned by the Society of Friends. Lay's physical appearance – he was a little person – served to increase his marginalisation.[50]

In the Civil Rights Movement of the twentieth century, Quakers also played a role, especially Bayard Rustin who was Lead Organiser of the 1963 March for Jobs and Freedom and whose interstate journey known as the 'Journey of Reconciliation' is widely regarded as the first 'freedom ride'. Solidarity funding was provided, Quaker Meeting Houses were made available for civil-rights meetings, individual members took part in most of the major campaigns and Friends provided opportunities for desegregated education. When Martin Luther King's *Letter from a Birmingham Jail* was smuggled out of prison in 1963 it was published by the American Friends Service Committee who distributed 100,000 copies. King later wrote that in his experience 'there are very few Quakers who are prejudiced from a racial point of view'. But Quakers were not immune from racial inequality. Both Quaker Schools and Meetings dragged their feet in the journey to becoming more inclusive themselves.[51]

Although a much smaller community in South Africa, Friends were nevertheless active throughout the struggle against apartheid by publicising injustices, acting as mediators and – in response to the forced removals of non-white South Africans – establishing the Cape Town Peace Centre. Some of the solidarity was financial, for example, Friends helped support projects led by Winnie Mandela and Steve Biko. Internationally, Quakers responded to the call for a global boycott of apartheid goods; in the process breaking ties with the Quaker-founded bank Barclays which had proven recalcitrant in its connections to the country. As they had with Martin Luther King, they also nominated Desmond Tutu for the Nobel Peace Prize repeatedly until he won.

Perhaps the most influential Quaker role was played by the activist Nozizwe Madlala-Routledge, a leader of the Natal Organisation of Women who campaigned for the African National Congress and South African Communist Party. Although neither the ANC nor SACP ruled out armed insurrection, Madlala-Routledge herself did. She acted on this conviction by co-leading campaigns against conscription in the country. After a decade of nonviolent activism – for which she was jailed three times – she was appointed to the committee that helped negotiate the end of apartheid and drafted the post-apartheid constitution. She stood for election in the first post-apartheid elections and was later appointed as a deputy minister in the Ministry of Defence – probably the only Quaker pacifist in history to be appointed to such a position.

Her story raises an important question: How is it that pacifists can participate in movements that have both nonviolent and armed components?

Questions of solidarity

The anti-slavery movement was by no means exclusively nonviolent and strands within it argued that only armed insurrection by enslaved people would end the injustice of slavery. In 1859 abolitionist rebel John Brown led an attempt to seize weapons from the federal armoury in order to equip such a movement. Several people were killed and Brown's men were forced to flee. Although Brown was neither a Quaker nor a pacifist, Friends wrote to Brown in prison affirming his intentions if not his methods, and during his trial his wife Mary Brown stayed with Quaker campaigners.[52]

The question of solidarity in a movement that employs a diversity of tactics was posed again in the 1960s when the foundation of the Black Panther Party brought new methods of resistance to the Civil Rights Movement, including armed patrols to dissuade policemen from acting violently towards black people. Whilst in sympathy with the goals, the method of carrying guns represented a block for many of those who had been active in the nonviolent movement. Some took their activism elsewhere – in particular the growing movement against the war in Vietnam. Others invited Black Panther members to gatherings, including Quaker Meetings, to help them understand one-another better.

In Baltimore, local Friends assisted with a Panther-led Breakfast Programme for local children. It was Philadelphia Friends who went furthest. Interested in 'What love can do' the Meeting supported a clinic, a community food market and a youth centre in partnership with local Panthers. In 1970 they provided their Arch Street Meeting House as a sanctuary during the Black Panthers' Convention and provided 150 volunteer observers in an effort to help the convention occur peacefully, at a time when black activists risked unprovoked attack by the FBI and police. Whilst emphasising their continued commitment to nonviolent solutions, these conversations led to the American Friends Service Committee nationally taking the step of speaking out with others against the government's brutal repression of Panther activity. It was an unusual step for a white-majority group, especially at a time when the FBI chief had labelled the Black Panther Party 'the greatest threat to the internal security of the country'.[53]

Interviewed in prison when falsely accused of aiding an armed attack, Black Panther supporter Angela Davis was asked about violence. Her reply was compelling:

> I grew up in Birmingham Alabama. Some very good friends of mine were killed by bombs, bombs that were planted by racists. From the time I was very small I remember the sounds of bombs exploding. I remember our house shaking. Bull Connor would often get on the radio and make statements like 'n****** have moved into a white neighbourhood, we'd better expect some bloodshed tonight.' And sure enough there would be bloodshed...I mean that's why when someone asks me about violence I just find it incredible, because what it means is that the person asking that question has absolutely no idea what black people have gone through.[54]

Different in different contexts, the challenge is an important one. For the former US Fellowship of Reconciliation chair AJ Muste: 'So long as we are not dealing honestly and openly with this 90% of our problem, there is something ludicrous and perhaps hypocritical in condemning the 10% of violence employed by the rebels against oppression.'[55] Reflecting on his time with freedom movements in South Africa and Latin America, Peace Studies pioneer Adam Curle built on this:

> 'I have often been asked how we handle the fact that peacemaking involves having a relationship, often a close relationship, with people who are committed to violent solutions to their problems. Do we tell them we disapprove of what they are doing or urge them to repent and desist? And if we don't, how do we square this with our principles? For my part I reply that I would never presume to criticise people caught up in a situation I do not share with them for the way

in which they are responding to that situation.' Nevertheless, 'I explain that I do not believe in the use of violence as either effective or moral; my job is to try to help people who can see no alternative to violence to find a substitute.'[56]

Systemic Injustice

It would be foolish to believe that systemic inequality exists only in the past. As the Black Lives Matter movement has highlighted, people of colour in the US are more than twice as likely to be shot by police as white people. In Britain you are more than three times as likely to be stopped and searched if you are black. Meanwhile better paid management jobs remain dominated by white people who hold nearly 95% of such positions.

Challenging such injustice isn't simply about co-opting people of colour into an unjust arrangement. As Reni Eddo-Lodge writes 'Equality is fine as a transitional demand, but it's dishonest not to recognise it for what it is: the easy route. There's a difference between saying "we want to be included" and saying "We want to reconstruct your exclusive system".'[57]

But for all of the progress of liberation movements, that exclusive system seems well intact. Some have seen the election of Donald Trump as United States President as an aberration. For others his election is the outworking of an unequal and imbalanced society.[58] By the time you read these words, the presidency of Trump may well be history. If it is I can only hope that the values that he represents will have been abandoned too. Creating a more equal society means more than swapping the people at the top. Preparing for peace involves dismantling the racist, sexist, disablist, homophobic and anti-working-class systems that socialise some people in to violent ideas and allow those people to gain political power. Part of that involves investigating the economic dynamics which entrench inequality. The journey to peace and to justice is also the journey to a nonviolent economy.

Chapter 7

Towards a nonviolent economy

On 14 June 2017, people in Britain woke up to the news of a fire in West London in the Grenfell Tower housing block. Even as the fire was still smouldering, members of the residents' association explained their repeated warnings about fire safety, which had gone unheeded by the local authority. More than 70 people were reported dead and a further 70 injured. Overwhelmingly they were working-class people, mostly from black, Asian and ethnic minority groups. The borough they lived in was the most unequal in Britain.

The disaster was an avoidable tragedy and had been the subject of multiple warnings both in specifics and in general. The slow process of privatisation over the past three decades had left local authorities ill-equipped to manage social housing and, in the case of Grenfell Tower, managed only by an arms-length organisation. Building regulations had been weakened. To intensify problems, local authority budgets had been slashed under the policy of austerity, providing difficulties for protecting communities in even the most dedicated councils. The fire was the result of the combined effects.[59]

In the shadow of such a disaster the link between a concern for peace and a concern for a fairer economy should be clear. More people died in the Grenfell fire than in all of the terrorist attacks on British soil of the past decade put together. Whether the result of design or neglect, there is no doubt that the effects of an unfair economy are profoundly violent.

But the violence of economic policy goes far beyond housing. In 2017 the campaigner Linda Burnip of the Disabled People Against Cuts campaign wrote that the process of restricting funds to those relying on financial support from the state had led to thousands of unnecessary claimant deaths as people have fallen into debt and become more physically and/or mentally ill.[60] Attempted suicides increase following benefit cuts. [61] Reductions in support for the vulnerable makes more people homeless, and leads to more people dying on the streets.[62]

A concern for the effects of economic injustice sheds light on the decisions of those politicians who spend money that could protect the lives of people at home on taking the lives of people abroad instead. The class dynamic continues in to the armed forces: Army recruitment targets working-class people, who are more likely to be killed than their middle-class colleagues.[63] A great many former-soldiers become homeless, and are in urgent need of medical help to assist with post-traumatic stress disorder (PTSD) amongst other disabilities and conditions that derive from war.[64]

Global Inequality

Taking a global view, the violent effects of economic inequality are even starker. Hundreds of millions of people worldwide subsist on poverty pay and women consistently earn less than men. The estimates of numbers of people who die each day from preventable causes are almost too big to conceptualise. The amount of rich people's money diverted away from social services into off-shore tax havens can only be guessed at, precisely because of the lack of transparency that governments of richer countries have not yet sufficiently used their powers to address. Meanwhile just eight billionaires (all male) are between them richer than half of the world's population.[65]

Global inequality is not the natural order of things. It is the product of centuries of wars and colonial conquest. These have set up economic dynamics through which wealth flows from what are now the poorer parts of the world to what are now the richer parts of the world. Sometimes this can be forgotten when it falls from the headlines. But sometimes events happen that make it necessary for everyone to stop and think.

In 2012, 124 people were killed and more than 200 injured in a fire at a garment factory in Bangladesh. The factory produced clothes for, amongst others, C&A, Wal-Mart and the US Marines. In 2013 more than 1000 people – most of them female garment workers – were killed when another building in the country collapsed. Low wages make people unsafe. It isn't only the need of all humans to achieve the basic dignity of a home, food, education, healthcare and savings. Low wages lead to people being unable to risk the loss of income from refusing dangerous conditions.[66]

Even when people do struggle for their rights there can be danger. In the same year, people in South Africa working as miners of platinum used in tablets and smart phones went on strike in calls for a reasonable wage. They were shot down by armed 'security forces' working with managers. The company – successor to the colonial era London and Rhodesia Mining and Land Company – is listed on the London Stock Exchange and is British owned. Two hundred years after the end of British rule and 20 years after the end of apartheid, the violent dynamics continue.

Peace and climate justice

Where natural resource extraction is most intense exploitation and violence are most intense too. In Nigeria, successive governments have enjoyed Western support in return for the protection of oil facilities, despite complicity in abuses of environmental defenders. In Sudan and South Sudan, conflict over oil has been a major factor in a war that has taken thousands of lives. In the Middle East, the Iran-Iraq war, first Gulf War and Iraq War have all been labelled wars for oil.

And still there is a yet deadlier outcome: The extraction and burning of fossil fuels in particular has led to so much waste carbon dioxide being trapped in the lower atmosphere that the global temperature has increased and the weather is becoming more and more extreme. The effects include rising sea levels, melting glaciers, increasing drought in some places and more intense flooding in others.

Both globally and within richer countries, the effects of climate change are distributed unequally. Richer people do most of the consuming and most of the production of carbon-dioxide, whilst being most insulated from the effects. The places where people are affected by the extraction process tend to be areas where people are poorer. Less privileged people also tend to live where the risks of extreme weather are greatest, and are the most vulnerable when crisis hits. Climate change isn't only a product of poor foresight. It is an intensification of the violence of inequality.

Nearly 2000 people were killed in the 2005 Hurricane Katrina which devastated New Orleans – a city in which the majority of people are African-American. Following decades of decline in public investment, government infrastructure that should have protected the city from the inflow of water didn't hold. As the crisis hit, the government agencies which should have been responsible for responding failed too. People were left without food and water for days. The resultant taking of provisions from local shops led to a racially tinged panic in parts of the media. Checkpoints were then set up to contain people in flooded areas. Police officers shot at unarmed black civilians.

Even the eventual relief operation was militarised. The journalist Naomi Klein was in the city when the National Guard arrived to organise the evacuation, writing later 'it was done with a level of aggression and ruthlessness that was hard to fathom. Soldiers pointed machine guns at residents as they boarded buses, providing no information about where they were being taken'.[67]To make matters worse, many of the very same private companies who have profited from providing 'security services' on sites of fossil fuel extraction and from middle-eastern wars for oil, look set to cash-in on the demand for armed private protection in the context of climate change.

Equality is good for us all

If at this point you are still entertaining the idea that pacifism has anything to do with passivity or is restricted to questions of war, listen out after an average Quaker Meeting for Worship. The chances are there will be an appeal for one organisation or another: Maybe Quaker Social Action, Quaker Homeless Action, Quaker Voluntary Action or the Earth Quaker Action Team. Perhaps you'll be invited to a protest or vigil to draw attention to an injustice that needs bringing into the light. Get into conversation and you'll most likely find people engaged in an earnest effort to understand the root causes of injustice. As part of this, the process of commissioning, supporting and engaging with research is part of the Quaker testimony to peace.

Perhaps the most influential book about equality of recent years is *The Spirit Level* by Kate Pickett and Richard Wilkinson. Their argument: That based on data across comparable countries, more equal countries have higher life expectancies, higher rates of mental health, higher rates of educational attainment and higher rates of recycling, alongside lower levels of conflict, imprisonment and homicide. In other words, one of the most effective ways to reduce violence and protect the environment is to create a more equal economy.[68]

Sometimes the decision facing societies has been presented as a false choice; between people and the environment. *The Spirit Level* revealed a new insight: that beyond a certain point, continually increasing consumption (measured as economic growth) stops bringing increases in happiness, life expectancy, or levels of well-being. In contrast, increasing equality does.

So, does being a pacifist necessitate being a socialist? It's true that the movements have developed together, demonstrated most influentially in the life of British Labour Party co-founder

Keir Hardie, who saw both as direct out-workings of his Christian beliefs, and who called on workers to refuse to go to war with one-another. But not everyone would agree. Inspired by the examples of ethical entrepreneurs and fair-trade pioneers some suggest that principled and philanthropic businesses can be harbingers of a fairer and more functional market economy, labelled by one writer 'Quakernomics'.[69]

What can be said for sure is that whilst pacifists often lean to the political left, the left is by no means exclusively pacifist. No discussion of economic violence can be complete without the acknowledgement of the masses lost to famine in Russia during the rule of Joseph Stalin and in China during the time of Chairman Mao, as well as the ecological catastrophes and disappearances that occurred under Communist rule. The exact numbers of casualties are disputed and will most likely never be known. What is clear is that the label of socialist is by no means an automatic guarantee of a nonviolent economy.

The Quaker concern for equality reaches back to the earliest days of the movement – even earlier indeed than the testimony to peace. But today it is still as front-of-mind as ever. How a fair economic system might look is at present the subject of more than 50 reading groups at Quaker Meetings across Britain, informed by a series of pamphlets supporting Friends and others to envision the New Economy. As Britain Yearly Meeting declared in 2015 'we are restless to take corporate action to change the unequal, unjust world in which we live. We are also called to be a community of Friends as a Yearly Meeting, pushed towards the important things we can only do together. We have a body of experience we can draw on and maintain. We are in this for the long haul.'[70]

Chapter 8

Never again?

When I was in my teens, my only dilemma of violence was in the school playground. Each of my grandfathers had a far greater question to consider: How to respond to the outbreak of World War Two. Would it be better to join up with the army without control over what they would be ordered to do? Or would it be better to join in with an independent ambulance unit, a humanitarian operation or an autonomous action group?

Each of my grandfathers responded differently, according to their abilities and experience. My step-grandfather joined the British army early; travelling as a mechanic as part of the first foray into France and evacuated at Dunkirk. My paternal grandfather, who began attending Quaker meetings later in life, had sought to build relations with German peace groups before the war began, but became disillusioned and signed up to work providing the British Army with supplies. My mother's father – already an active member of his Quaker Meeting – registered as a conscientious objector before joining the pacifist Friends Ambulance Unit, was assigned to France and Germany during the war and transferred after the war's end to the Friends Relief Service to work with refugees.

Modern-day pacifists may well ask themselves what we would have done, or indeed we might be asked by others. Until we are in the moment we cannot know for sure. There is though, a bigger question which is perhaps the most important question for any person of conscience to consider: how can genocide and crimes against humanity can be prevented from happening in the first place? Over 60 million people were killed in World War Two, including six million Jews as well as gypsies, communists, dissenters, people of colour, homosexual people, non-gender conforming people and disabled people who were exterminated by the Nazi Party in the Holocaust. We now know that the rise of fascism, the Holocaust and the Second World War were all avoidable catastrophes. How could any society allow such systematised slaughter to prevail?

To answer that question means looking before the 1930s and beyond Germany to the brutal process of racist dehumanisation across Europe, which led to the cultural acceptance that some people can be massacred by others. For decades before the outbreak of war, decisions could have been taken by governments to lay the groundwork for peace and for justice. Instead the path to genocide and war was set. As we say never again, so too we must never forget.

The road to genocide

Perhaps the first great philosopher to investigate the conditions that led to Nazism was the Jewish German-American Hannah Arendt. In her 1948 work *The Origins of Totalitarianism* she observed that the fundamental aspects of European colonialism 'appear so close to totalitarian phenomena of the twentieth century that it may be justifiable to consider the whole period a preparatory stage for coming catastrophes'.[71]

Amongst these were atrocities perpetrated in German controlled-territories. But they were not alone. The term 'concentration camp' was first widely used to describe the British practice of imprisoning Afrikaner women and children in the course of the second Boer war. The practice was virtually unknown in Britain until exposed by humanitarian campaigners.

The most wide-reaching colonial mass killing was the Belgian extermination of nearly half the population of the Congo – up to thirteen million people between 1885 and 1908. When US church minister George Washington Williams discovered what was happening he was so shocked that he coined a new phrase – a crime against humanity. The campaign was invigorated by the efforts of the journalist E.D. Morel. In his later writings he warned that competition between the European colonisers could lead to world war. But the warning went unheeded.

On the outbreak of the 'Great War', a new organisation was founded called the No Conscription Fellowship to support British people who refused to fight. E.D. Morel became the staff member to another anti-war organisation, the Union for Democratic Control, which campaigned for parliamentary control over foreign policy, negotiations to form an organisation to help prevent future conflicts, and – prophetically –for a peace agreement that 'neither humiliates the defeated nation nor artificially rearranges frontiers as this might provide a cause for future wars'.

The British Government could have avoided another war by listening. Instead many peace activists, including Morel, were imprisoned. The Treaty of Versailles imposed upon Germany at the end of World War One was so punitive that it became a major factor in the rise of the Nazi Party. It also helps explain the support that non-fascist Germans later gave their government in World War Two, as they sought to relieve the next generation from a repetition of the kinds of conditions imposed by the victors of World War One. The alarm was raised at the time by those humanitarian workers able to get into Germany.[72] But once again they were ignored.

Weapons capability became even more deadly when the tactic of aerial bombardment was developed by the British in Iraq, led by Arthur 'Bomber' Harris, who in 1920 boasted presciently that 'within 45 minutes a full-sized village…can be practically wiped out and a third of its inhabitants killed or injured'. Those actions have been reported as helping the Nazis develop their ideas about 'The Total War'.[73]

Between the wars, peace campaigners suggested systems to support all nations to disarm, proposed aviation should be controlled and that aerial bombing should be prohibited.

Instead Britain, France and the US opted to continue the fighting by sending troops to join the civil war against the newly revolutionary government of Russia.[74]

As Italy's fascist government threatened to invade Ethiopia in 1935 campaigners called for bans on oil exports to Italy, but these were not heeded by the US, France or UK. When fascists came to power in Spain in 1936 they received tacit support from the British Government, seen as preferable to the left-wing alternative in the country.

Across Europe and North America violent anti-Semitism was on the rise. In Britain the Quaker and Jewish communities worked together to assist Jews to escape from Germany, culminating in the 'Kindertransport' evacuation of 1938 when 10,000 Jewish children were assisted to safety. Whilst widely celebrated today, this represented an exception. Many other Jewish adults – including the children's parents – were required by the UK Government to stay in Germany where they would be subjected to the horrors of the Nazi regime. On the outbreak of war in 1939 the scheme was forced to end. Thereafter the UK Government turned away, restricted the movement of, and even deported many German-born Jews as 'enemy aliens'. These developments were mirrored in the US. Amongst the many refused visas to the United States, was the teenage Jewish diarist Anne Frank.

Even in the choices made during the war itself, actions that could have saved people from the gas chambers were de-prioritised, against actions that took ordinary people's lives. The allies did not act on their capability to disrupt the concentration camps, even when asked to do so by Jewish groups, seeing doing so as distraction.[75] German documents of the time reveal an even more uncomfortable possibility. The decision to embark on the 'Final Solution' – the bloody attempt which began in 1941 to murder all of the Jews in the territories it controlled – would not have been possible without the cover of the war itself.[76]

Civil Resistance

Observing the trial of the Nazi Adolf Eichmann in Jerusalem, who had overseen the transportation of people to the concentration camps, Hannah Arendt commented on what she saw as the 'banality of evil'.[77] She noted that the defendant seemed to believe that he was just doing his job. As with the trial of other Nazis at Nuremberg, the assumption of the hearing – now built into international law – is that if a person knows something to be wrong they should refuse to obey orders.

And some people did. In Norway thousands of teachers refused to participate in the identification of Jewish students, which led to thousands of people being saved. In Denmark a largely nonviolent programme of non-cooperation and sabotage made their country ungovernable by their Nazi occupiers and thousands of Jews were smuggled out to Sweden, whose government welcomed them.[78] Many Bulgarians found ways of resisting their anti-Semitic rulers' plans, to the extent that the deportation of Jews had to be abandoned there. So too in Finland, non-military means were used to safeguard the lives of almost all of the country's Jews. In France the remote parish of le Chambon-sur-Lignon helped an unknowable number of Jews and political dissidents from the threat of deportation.[79] Where people had the means to do so, there were stories of church people providing baptism certificates as a means of protection, even when a baptism hadn't taken place.[80]

In Germany there was only one mass protest by non-Jewish Germans against the deportation of Jews. A street gathering led by women on Berlin's Rosenstrasse led to thousands of Jews who were married to non-Jewish Germans being released, as the authorities sought to avoid the negative publicity.[81] Although the method was as yet underdeveloped, where nonviolent civil resistance was tried it had a remarkable rate of success. But despite the many stories of bravery, yet another great tragedy of the Second World War was that such non-co-operation was not sufficiently developed to become more widespread.

Part of that tragedy was that the major institutions of society did not do all they could to stymie the Nazi atrocities. This included the principal German churches whose membership between them spanned most of the population. Early on some Bishops prohibited church members from joining the Nazi party, but they dropped the ban after Hitler declared Christianity the foundation for German values. Some conservative church leaders supported Hitler's rise and promoted a twisted form of the faith. When others refused to do so, dissenting church leaders were arrested. In response the Confessing Church grew underground. Some of its members engaged in acts of bravery, including in assisting Jews. Even this church though was not free of anti-Semitism. The *kirchenkampf* (church struggle) that ensued was principally an internal struggle which stopped short of action to challenge the regime.[82]

Some international corporations also became complicit by providing the regime with resources. In 1933 IBM made a deal with the Nazis to supply the punch-card technology that would enable the systematic identification of people who would be killed. Ford Motors provided military equipment until 1941 when the US entered the war. Standard Oil of New Jersey – known today as Exxon-Mobil – helped keep the fuel flowing even after the US had joined the war.[83]

No authoritarian ruler can sustain their control if the sources of their power are taken away. Without fuel, without equipment, without people and without legitimacy, no government of any type can continue for long. As Gene Sharp observed, if a regime lacks 'at least passive support from the general population and his/her agents, the most powerful dictator in the world becomes just another crackpot with dreams of domination'.[84]

How do we remember?

How we remember the Second World War influences the

decisions we make in the present. If we accept, without question, a simplistic narrative in which the war was a glorious battle between good and evil, we are equipped only with the basis for the ongoing justification for violent acts since. If we dig deeper, and see the rise of the Nazi party as a catastrophe that could have been avoided, we begin to equip ourselves with ideas about how genocide and crimes against humanity can be stopped before they start. To do so with integrity we have to remember those acts that could be considered crimes against humanity committed by Allied troops.

The German bombing of Coventry flattened thousands of buildings and killed more than 500 people. In response, Arthur Harris led bombing raids on Dresden, followed by further attacks on other populous cities. The attacks caused the deaths of, by some estimates, more than half a million people. The objective of breaking the resolve of the German working class was not achieved. But the tactic was nevertheless extended. In 1945 the United States army firebombed Tokyo, killing 100,000 people in a single night. In the same year, the only nuclear bombs ever to have been used in war were dropped on the civilian populations of Hiroshima and Nagasaki in Japan. More than 150,000 ordinary people were killed. As the war came to a close and Berlin was occupied, thousands of German women were raped by Allied soldiers.[85]

When the Second World War ended, many said such a war must never be repeated. The United Nations was formed in 1945 as a forum where international disputes could be negotiated rather than fought over. In 1948 it agreed the Universal Declaration of Human Rights and in 1951 the Refugee Convention – each of them landmark treaties providing a level of international protection to ordinary citizens from the actions of their governments. At the same time, discussions leading to the creation of the modern-day European Union also began – an institution that has played no small part in the prevention of another European war for which it was awarded the Nobel Peace Prize in 2012. Since 1945 there has not been genocide on the scale of the Holocaust. But the words *never again* still carry a heavy poignancy. In Cambodia in 1975, Rwanda in 1994 and today in the Yemen, genocide and mass killing resembling genocide has continued with the knowledge, the acquiescence and the military equipment of countries who were victors of World War Two. This was by no means because of a newfound commitment to non-intervention. The victors of World War Two continued fighting, but this time with one-another. Only five years after the end of the war in Europe, tensions between communist and capitalist countries erupted in Korea, where the ensuing war took more than 3 million people's lives. It was followed soon after by the Vietnam War, which killed as many people again. As wars continued, the Second World War became less an example of the horrors of violence, and increasingly became used as the justification for more. As the US prepared to escalate its involvement in Vietnam, the President and his Security Advisor dismissed offers of peace talks by comparing the North Vietnamese Government to the Nazis.

The analogy was used to justify assassinations and imprisonments such as the US-sponsored killing of Congo's first democratic Prime Minister Patrice Lumumba.[86]So too in Ghana: When the British colonial governor jailed the independence leader Kwame Nkrumah he labelled him 'our local Hitler'.[87]Following an anti-colonial uprising in Kenya, the British rulers forced more than a million people into detention camps where tens of thousands of people died. Despite the racism, violence and white-supremacy underpinning the colonial occupation, some among the British saw their actions through the lens of the war of the previous decade. For example, a widely read piece in *The Telegraph* described independence leader Jomo Kenyatta as 'A small scale African Hitler' and continued 'there are grievances of course. Germany had grievances too. Appeasing Hitler did not cure them, nor will appeasing the Kikuyu'. [88]

And so it continues in the twenty-first century. As the US and UK embarked on their wars in Afghanistan in 2001, Iraq in 2003, Libya in 2011 and Syria in 2015, political rhetoric seemed still to be fighting the war against Germany. Even when the analogies are wildly inaccurate, they are repeated precisely because they work to build public support for violence. Nations once went to war declaring God was on their side. Now they declare that Hitler is on the other.

The rhetoric of fighting Hitler has even been used without irony by modern-day xenophobic and far-right groups, who have variously compared their election campaigns to the Battle of Britain,[89]appropriated the Red Poppy (a symbol of remembrance)[90] and advocated shooting immigrants because 'It's our border, they're invading us' and 'stopping Hitler was worth the price'.[91] In the UK's 2016 referendum on whether to leave the European Union the EU was so frequently compared to Nazi Germany by campaigners to leave, that the German Ambassador had to ask people to stop.[92] The rhetoric spilled on to the street where references to the Second World War have played a role in racist hate crime[93] which itself rose sharply in the wake of the referendum result.

To learn from history, we need to learn about history and especially about how wars and intolerance can be averted. When violent xenophobia is advanced in the name of a war against a violently xenophobic regime, it must be cause to stop and think. Surely the worst way to honour those who died in the Second World War is to carry on killing in their name.

The first step to peace

On 11 November at 11am Britain stops for two minutes to commemorate the dead. Some people wear red poppies to remember Allied troops. Others wear white poppies to remember the civilians as well as the soldiers killed by war. Sometimes the ceremonies make space for reflection on how war might be reduced. Increasingly often they glorify, glamorise and promote the wars that are happening now.

What is always the case is that, for me at least, those two minutes feel like too short a time to consider the millions lost, too short to ask what it is that we might each do to prevent such tragedies and too short to receive a reply. Too short to learn about the peacemakers hidden from history and too short to unlearn those attitudes absorbed through our culture that make us more likely to make the same errors again.

That is, I suppose, at least part of the reason why I go to Quaker Meeting. Remembering war and considering peace deserves more than two minutes a year. To remember with integrity involves asking how a culture imbued with injustice can be rethought and remade for the better. It's a consideration of such magnitude that it takes time and can't be engaged with alone. When opportunities arise to change things, a Quaker community is a group with which to do so.

As we begin the process of contemplation, George Fox had some practical advice:

'Do not simply look at the temptations, confusions and corruptions of the world, but at the light that discovers them. For looking down at corruption and distraction, you are swallowed up in it; but looking at the light that discovers them, you will see over them and with the same light stand against them.'[94]

'There,' he said 'is the first step to peace.'

Chapter 9

But what would you do if...

And then there will be one more question, or maybe a series of questions that all start in the same way: 'But what would you do if...'

A longstanding peacemaker once advised me that the starting point for pacifism is to recognise that we all have the capacity for violence. We can probably all recall moments when we have acted violently or come close to doing so. Probably too there are moments when a quick decision to act peacefully has helped calm a tense situation or prevent its escalation.

Much of the time our options are restricted. If we are mugged at knifepoint in an empty street, it may be that the best choice is to hand over the money. Even if we have a weapon with us, using it would most likely make the situation more unsafe. After the danger has passed we might reflect on the courses of action that might have been available. Every situation is different. Sometimes peacemakers have found creative nonviolent responses to threats.

There is a story about the prison reformer Elizabeth Fry, who staying in Bristol in the course of her work saw a boot protruding from under her bed. Aware of the danger of the situation and the limited options open to her she knelt down and prayed out loud for the intruder until he emerged. When he did she asked him about his story, supplied him with some money and ensured that he made it out of the hotel without attracting the attention of the porter.[95]

Non-violence theorist Angie O'Gorman tells a similar story: She was woken by her bedroom door being kicked in and the sounds of a man swearing and moving towards her. As the house was empty and the phone was downstairs she had to think quickly. Realising that if he raped her then both would be damaged, she felt confidence to engage in conversation, beginning by asking the time and continuing by asking how he got into the house. The conversation extended to each of their financial difficulties, until she felt it was safe to ask him to leave. When he said he had no place to go, she replied she would give him a clean set of sheets but he would have to make his own bed downstairs. She sat up in bed shaking for the rest of the night. After breakfast in the morning he left.[96]

Nonviolence by no means rules out physical intervention such as breaking up a fight or pulling an attacker away from a victim. But never should such instances be conflated with killing. The Catholic social activist Dorothy Day tells a story of an incident in a house of hospitality. A guest – himself a victim of World War One – picked up a breadknife and a crucifix and announced he would kill another person present. Day writes in her memoir: 'Another woman and I seized him, forcing him to drop the knife. We could not hold him however, and after he had hurled a gallon can of vegetables at Arthur and smashed a hole in the wall, we restrained him for long enough to allow Arthur to escape.'[97]

You don't need to be a pacifist to find alternatives to killing. The Black Panther Assata Shakur tells in her memoir of being lured as a teenager to an older boy's house where he and his friends attempted to gang rape her. After hearing the boy ask the others to be careful with an ashtray because it was his mother's house, Assata took her cue. She picked up a vase and threw it at the wall, then grabbed a lamp, which she said she would throw at the mirror if anyone touched her. Her assailants started to leave until only the first boy remained. She told him that if he didn't want his mum's house being smashed up he'd need to go next door with her and speak to a neighbour. The plan worked, they went next door – Assata still holding the lamp – and she got away to safety.[99]

More recently there's the account of the worshippers at Finsbury Park Mosque who in 2017 were subjected to a terrorist van-ramming attack on their way home from prayers. As the perpetrator emerged from his van shouting 'I want to kill all Muslims' worshippers restrained him, sat on him and called the police so he could serve a proper trial. The imam Mohammed Mahmud who was credited with calming the situation reflected later 'It's almost a back-handed compliment when they say "hero imam". The norm is that Muslims would have lynched this guy and killed him? No, the norm is to do what I did.'[98]

The attacks amongst others resurfaced the debate about the extent to which police should carry guns. In Britain the majority of police are unarmed, and when consulted on whether to routinely arm officers, police workers have explained that the carrying of firearms does not lead to reductions in violent crime and puts police workers themselves at greater risk. A comparison of the US and UK shows they are right. In the US where police routinely carry guns, the rates of homicide and the killing of police is far higher.

The scale of the problem made world headlines in 2018 when an attacker broke in to a school in Florida and killed 17 staff and students. In response, Donald Trump suggested that teachers should carry guns too. It fell upon the teenage survivors to make it their mission to prevent the next school massacre by publicly explaining what the government and the gun lobby are yet to understand: that the most effective way to stop violent gun crime is to identify the causes and to cut off the supply of weapons in the first place.[100]

So it is that across the world, people and communities find creative ways to respond to violence non-violently. It might sound trite to say we challenge violence with peace. But we don't fight fire with fire. We douse it with water. The sustained strategic pursuit of peace with justice is the only effective long-term answer to violence. That is the vocation of the pacifist.

What canst thou say?

There's an old Quaker story about when George Fox first asked Margaret Fell about her beliefs. She quoted various writings in her response, to which Fox replied 'But what canst *thou* say?' I promised I would tell you why I am a pacifist, and wonder if I hear you enquire something similar: 'you have told me about the pacifism of others, but what can *you* say. You still haven't told me what *you* would do if...'

My pacifist journey began after a fight on the last day of school. Shortly afterwards I moved to college and thought I had left my problems behind. That was, until the following bonfire night, on a visit to the local fireworks display. Half way through I went to the urinals. Then I felt a knee in my back then sharp pain on the back of my head. 'It's Gee you f****** poof'. I zipped up my trousers, and turned around. There were the boys who had taunted us through school. I felt scared. But I didn't hit back. Despite the circumstance, I felt calm. I walked to find the friend I'd arrived with and headed calmly out. The boys followed to the gate, then left us as we walked to the bus stop.

I'd already started getting involved in protest, by attending a rally against a law that prevented teachers from acknowledging the normality of homosexuality. There were drag queens in feathers and a blockade of a Stagecoach bus to highlight the company boss financing the other side of the argument. I'd joined towards the end of a long-running campaign and two years later the law was repealed. My role had been miniscule but I'd also seen how pressure could lead to change.

I began to learn more about nonviolent action and did training based on the workshops delivered for the civil rights movement. Half the group would role-play police or security services while the other half would practise staying calm if antagonised. The training worked. In the course of different protests since, I've been stopped and searched, beaten by police, rammed by a van, charged by horses, illegally detained in police-imposed 'kettles' and on one occasion arrested and tried – ironically on charges of breach of the peace. Some of those protests played a role in winning change. Others form a part of struggles still ongoing. Never once in the course of any campaign have I ever hit back.

Through writing I try to tell stories of people who have overcome injustice with nonviolence. More recently I've begun a process of trying to consider how being white, male and straight has endowed me with certain privileges, and how to be as useful as possible in the circumstances whilst trying not to reinforce inequalities. In particular I try to raise such conversations with others who share my characteristics, in order to think through together how best to stand against oppression.

In my spiritual life I try to reflect on the implications of the conviction that God resides within everyone, everywhere without exception. I ask for the strength to stay calm, to keep going, to examine myself for those behaviours which carry the seeds of war and be able to hear the things I might not want to hear. I ask for the resolve to change those systems I believe to be harmful, and to do so in a way where I carry some peace in my heart. In communities and spaces I help host or hold, I ask what can be done to support each person to express their full humanity. Most difficult of all, I try to hold open the possibility that I could be mistaken.

A few years ago, I was asked for a publication what the Peace Testimony means to me. I replied that I see it as a commitment to placing spanners in systems that would otherwise result in violence. I feel that I could have gone further though. Testimony is about more than our actions. To give testimony is to offer witness to the truth as we experience it.

At the core of my truth is a heartfelt conviction that each person has within us an inner light, manifested in the promptings of love and of truth. With practice, peace can exist within us. When we gather it exists among us. By building with others a movement for liberation, that peace can spill out to the world.

References

Chapter 1: Why I am a pacifist

1:   This idea is explored by Mark Kurlansky in *Nonviolence: the History of a Dangerous Idea*, Vintage, 2007.

2:   David Gee, *Holding Faith: Creating Peace in a Violent World*, Quaker Books, 2011.

3:   Kristina Keefe-Perry, 'Why I am not a Pacifist', *Quaker Speak*, http://quakerspeak.com/why-im-not-pacifist/

4:   'Shalomist' is the word suggested by Kristina Keefe-Perry. 'Pacificist' has been suggested to denote a belief that makes the abolishing of war the ultimate goal but allows for violence in the short term where it is unavoidable in pursuit of peace.

5:   A similar case was made by Emmanuel Kant in his 1795 essay *Perpetual Peace*.

6:   George Fox quoted in *Quaker Faith and Practice* 24.01, Britain Yearly Meeting, 2009.

7:   Quoted in *Quaker Faith and Practice*, 19.46, Britain Yearly Meeting, 2009.

8:   The story also helps explain the comparatively successful attempts in Pennsylvania to model peaceful relationships, including with Native Americans and with other persecuted minorities who escaped there.

9:   Sylvia Pankhurst, 'What Is a Pacifist?' in *Woman's Dreadnought*, April 8, 1916. Martin Luther King 'Letter from a Birmingham Jail' in *The Autobiography of Martin Luther King*, edited by Clayborne Carson, Abacus, 1999.

10: Bayard Rustin, *Time on Two Crosses: The Collected Writings of Bayard Rustin*, Cleis Press, 2015. The title refers to Rustin's work against racism and homophobia. Despite his talent Bayard Rustin was forced to resign from the Southern

Christian Leadership Conference after being caught having sex with a man. He later suggested removing his name from an American Friends Service Committee pamphlet titled 'Speak Truth to Power' in case his co-authorship should undermine it.

11: One of the ways Quakers have done this is supporting the negotiated ends to armed conflicts, including in Zimbabwe, South Africa and Northern Ireland. In Geneva, Brussels and New York today, Quakers provide neutral spaces for citizens and representatives of different nations to meet, build bridges and address international tensions through dialogue.

Chapter 2: War is the greater evil

12: William Charles Braithwaite quoted in *Quaker Faith and Practice* 23.05, Britain Yearly Meeting, 2009.

13: The first of these figures comes from the Iraq Body Count survey. The second is from the polling organisation ORB

14: Leo Tolstoy, *What I Believe*, 1885, Chapter 4

15: Global Research, 'The US has killed more than 20 million people in 37 victim nations since the Second World War', first published 2015,https://www.globalresearch.ca/us-has-killed-more-than-20-million-people-in-37-victim-nations-since-world-war-ii/5492051?print=1

16: Leo Tolstoy, *What I Believe*, 1885, Chapter 4

Chapter 3: Thou shalt not kill

17: In *The Powers That Be* (Galilee, 1998) theologian Walter Wink suggests that in the context of the customs of the time a back-handed slap would be administered to a social inferior so to turn the other cheek would be to disrupt unjust hierarchies by inviting an assailant to slap with the forehand as they would for an equal. He suggests that other examples in the Sermon on the Mount such as giving away one's coat if sued, and walking for two miles if forced by a soldier to walk for one, would have had similar effects.

18: The early church also shared money and resources, anticipating on a smaller scale how the 'Kingdom of Heaven' might be. Quotes by early Christian leaders are from Mark Kurlansky, *Nonviolence: The History of a Dangerous Idea*, Vintage, 2007, chapter 2.

19: For the full text see https://www.archbishopofcanterbury. org/speaking-and-writing/speeches/archbishop-canter burys-speech-syria

20: Graça Machel's full speech can be read on the UNICEF website https://www.unicef.org/graca/patterns.htm

21: See for example Amnesty International, *War of Annihilation*, June 2018 https://www.amnesty.org/en/ latest/news/2018/06/syria-raqqa-in-ruins-and-civilians-devastated-after-us-led-war-of-annihilation/

22: Howard Zinn, *A People's History of the USA*, Harper Collins, reprinted 2009, Chapter 18

23: PR Watch, *How PR Sold the War in the Persian Gulf*, https:// www.prwatch.org/books/tsigfy10.html

24: Alfred Salter, 'Faith of a Pacifist' quoted in Graham Taylor, *Ada Salter: Pioneer of Ethical Socialism*, Laurence and Wishart, 2016

Chapter 4: The Power of Nonviolence

25: Erica Chenoweth and Maria J Stephan, *Why Civil Resistance Works: The Strategic Logic of Nonviolent Conflict*, Columbia University Press, 2011

26: For example, *The Politics of Nonviolent Action* (1973), *Gandhi as a political strategist* (1979), *Making Europe Unconquerable: The potential of Civilian Based Deterrence and Defence* (1985),

From Dictatorship to Democracy(1989), *The Anti-Coup* (2003), *Self Liberation* (with Jamila Raqib, 2010). Other influential theorists of why and how nonviolent struggle works include Reformed Church pastor Bart de Ligt and US Quakers George Lakey and Richard B Gregg who are referenced in Sharp's work.

27: Henry Thoreau, *On the Duty of Civil Disobedience, 1849*

28: From the Papers of Martin Luther King, Jr., Volume IV: *Symbol of the Movement*

29: Diane Nash, 'Nonviolent protest was the most important invention of the 20th Century', interview with *The Guardian*, 6 April 2017

30: This story is told in the 2014 feature film *Selma* in which Nash is a depicted as a character. Also depicted are Coretta Scott King, James Bevel, John Lewis and Martin Luther King amongst others.

31: See Sybil Morrison, *I Renounce War: The Story of the Peace Pledge Union*, PPU, 1962and Kate Hudson, *CND: Now More than Ever: The Story of a Peace Movement*, Vision, 2005

32: From a video posted August 28 2017, *Activist Dolores Huerta and filmmaker Peter Bratt on Gandhi and Cesar Chavez*. https:// kamlashow.com/2017/08/28/video-activist-dolores-huerta-and-filmmaker-peter-bratt-on-gandhi-cesar-chavez/

33: The story is told well in Ruaridh Arrow's 2011 documentary *How to Start a Revolution*.

34: Erica Chenoweth and Maria J Stephan, *Why Civil Resistance Works: The Strategic Logic of Nonviolent Conflict*, Columbia University Press, 2011

35: Michael Randle, Review of *Why Civil Resistance Works* for *Peace News*, July-August 2012

36: The word 'intersectionality' was coined by US academic Kimberlé Crenshaw to describe how different forms of inequality and oppression can reinforce one-another.

Chapter 5: Gender, sexuality and peace

37: Quaker Women's Group, *Swarthmore Lecture: Bringing the Invisible in to the Light,* Britain Yearly Meeting, 1986

38: World Health Organisation, reported by CNN, 20 June 2013, https://edition.cnn.com/2013/06/20/health/global-violence-women/index.html

39: Southbank Centre discussion, *Why Are Most Terrorists Men?,* https://www.southbankcentre.co.uk/whats-on/124095-why-are-most-terrorists-men-2017

40: Stonewall, *2018 Hate Crime Report,* https://www.stonewall.org.uk/comeoutforLGBT/lgbt-in-britain/hate-crime

41: Reuters, *2 in 5 Military Women Endure Sexual Trauma during Service,* August 2017 2015

42: Lucretia Mott, Elizabeth Pease, Sylvia Pankhurst, Jane Addams, Ada Salter, Emily Hobhouse and Emmeline Pethwick-Laurence were just some of the women who were prominent in both the women's suffrage and peace movements of the nineteenth and twentieth centuries.

43: Virginia Woolf, 'Three Guineas' in *The Collected Works of Virginia Woolf,* p. 861

44: Both quotes from J Todd Moye, *Ella Baker: Community Organiser of the Civil Rights Movement,* Rowman and Littlefield, 2015 (reprint), p. 90 and p. 98

45: Mary King and Casey Hayden, *Sex and Caste,* 18 November 1965. A similar case was made during the nineteenth century by the Quaker feminist and abolitionist Lucretia Mott after being having part of a group (which also included Anne Knight) who were excluded from ananti-slavery convention because of their gender. Mott's reflections are included in the Quaker Faith and Practice at 23.39 and 23.41

46: Gay in the 80s website www.gayinthe80s.com

47: Feminism and Nonviolence Study Group, *Piecing it Together,* 1983, available on War Resisters' International website

48: Reni Eddo-Lodge, *Why I'm No Longer Talking to White People About Race,* Bloomsbury, 2017.

Chapter 6: Pacifism and Anti-Racism

49: Angela Davis, *The Meaning of Freedom*, City Lights, 2012

50: Marcus Rediker, *The Fearless Benjamin Lay: The Quaker Dwarf who Became the First Revolutionary Abolitionist*, Beacon Press, 2017

51: See Vanessa Julye and Donna McDaniel, *Fit for Freedom Not for Friendship*, FGC, 2010. The Martin Luther King quote is from *The Autobiography of Martin Luther King*, edited by Clayborne Carson, Abacus, 1999, p. 149.

52: Vanessa Julye and Donna McDaniel, *Fit for Freedom Not for Friendship*, FGC, 2010. Chapter 5

53: Vanessa Julye and Donna McDaniel, *Fit for Freedom Not for Friendship*, FGC, 2010. Chapter 9

54: Angela Davis in *The Black Power Mixtape, 1967–1975*, dir. Goran Olsson.

55: AJ Muste quoted in Andrew Cornell, *Oppose and Propose: Lessons from Movement for a New Society*, AK Press, 2011, p. 131

56: Adam Curle quoted in *Quaker Faith and Practice*, 24.35, Britain Yearly Meeting, 2009.

57: Reni Eddo-Lodge, *Why I'm No Longer Talking to White People About Race,* Bloomsbury, 2017, p185

58: Naomi Klein, *No is Not Enough*, Allen Lane, 2017 pp. 9–10

Chapter 7: Towards a nonviolent economy

59: Gurpreet Bola, 'How Can We Help Prevent Tragedies like Grenfell?', *Quakers in Britain*, December 2017, http://www.quaker.org.uk/blog/preventing-grenfell-addressing-root-causes

60: Linda Burnip, 'Disabled People Oppose the Tories and Need Your Help', *New Internationalist*, 1 June 2017

61: e.g. May Bulman, 'Attempted Suicides by Disability Benefit Claimants more than Double after Introduction of Fit-To-Work Assessment', *The Independent*, 28 December 2017

62: e.g. Sarah Marsh and Patrick Greenfield, 'Deaths of UK Homeless People more than Double in Five Years', *The Guardian*, 11 April 2018

63: Chris Hughes, 'Young Soldiers from Working Class Backgrounds Most at Risk on Front Line, says Report', *The Mirror*, 28 October 2013

64: Patrick Christys, 'Is this ANY Way to Treat our Soldiers?', *The Express*, 23 March 2017

65: Oxfam, *An Economy for the 99%*, January 2017

66: War on Want, *Never Again: Making Factories Safe*, April 2014

67: Naomi Klein, 'How Power Profits from Disaster', *The Guardian*, 6 July 2017

68: Kate Pickett and Richard Wilkinson, *The Spirit Level: Why Equality is Better for Everyone*, Penguin, 2010. The Equality Trust was established with support from the Quaker-founded Joseph Rowntree Charitable Trust. Wilkinson later chaired Britain's first Fairness Commission. The story of this is told by Catherine West MP in her 2017 Swarthmore lecture *Faith in Politics?: Our Testament to Equality*.

69: Mike King, *Quakernomics: An Ethical Capitalism*, Anthem, 2014

70: Britain Yearly Meeting, Minute 36: 'Living out our Faith in the World', 2015

Chapter 8: Never again?

71: Hannah Arendt, *The Origins of Totalitarianism*, 1951, Schocken Books

72: Many of the British and US relief workers in Germany after

WW1 were Quakers, whose accounts – including those of Ruth Fry – have survived, and are reproduced as part of Julia Boyd's *Travellers in the Third Reich: The Rise of Fascism through the Eyes of Ordinary People*, Elliott and Thompson, 2017.Fry had earlier worked with Emily Hobhouse in exposing British atrocities in South Africa.

73: Pankaj Mishra, 'How Colonial Violence Came Home: The Ugly Truth of the First World War' in *The Guardian*, 10 November 2017

74: George Lansbury, *My Pilgrimage for Peace*, H Holt, 1938

75: Mark Kurlansky, *Non-Violence: The History of a Dangerous Idea*, Vintage, 2007

76: Explored in Gene Sharp, *Social Power and Political Freedom*, Porter Sargeant, 1980 and Mark Kurlansky, *Non-Violence: The History of a Dangerous Idea*, Vintage 2007

77: Hannah Arendt, *Eichmann in Jerusalem: A Report on the Banality of Evil*, Viking, 1963

78: Peter Ackerman and Jack Du Vall, *A Force More Powerful*, Palgrave MacMillan, 2001. The accompanying PBS documentary is available online. See also Walter Wink, *The Powers that Be*, Galilee, 1998, Chapter 8.

79: Caroline Moorehead, *Village of Secrets: Defying the Nazis in Vichy France*, Vintage, 2014

80: Amongst them were the Paris-based Maria Skobstova and Demetri Klepinin who were canonised as saints in 2004.

81: The Rosenstrasse demonstration, 1943, *The Holocaust Encyclopedia*, https://www.ushmm.org/wlc/en/article.php?ModuleId=10008064

82: The German Churches and the Nazi state, *The Holocaust Encyclopedia*, https://www.ushmm.org/wlc/en/article.php?ModuleId=10005206.In the absence of a wider nonviolent movement against the regime, the pastor and former pacifist Dietrich Bonhoeffer sought to help assassinate Hitler in 1944. He was killed in a concentration camp in 1945.

83: Charles Higham, *Trading with the Enemy: An Exposé of The Nazi-American Money-Plot 1933-1949*, Delacorte Press, 1983. Hitler described Henry Ford as 'my inspiration' and awarded him the highest German honour available to a non-German. ITT, General Motors and Coca-Cola were also amongst the companies who traded with the Nazis.

84: Gene Sharp, *The Politics of Non-Violent Action*, Porter Sargeant, 1973

85: Lucy Ash, 'The Rape of Berlin', *BBC News Magazine*, 1 July 2015, https://www.bbc.co.uk/news/magazine-32529679. One of the roles voluntarily taken on by Friends Ambulance Unit members after the end of the war was to stay in the houses of women who feared they would otherwise be raped.

86: Emmanuel Gerard, *Death in the Congo: Murdering Patrice Lumumba*, Harvard, 2015, p. 148

87: Martin Meredith, *The State of Africa: A History of 50 Years of Independence*, Free Press, 2005, p. 19

88: Elizabeth Huxley, *Letter to the Telegraph*, 1 November 1952, quoted in Anthony Clayton and Donald Cockfield Savage, *Government and Labour in Kenya 1895–1963*, Routledge, 1974

89: 'BNP Uses Polish Spitfire in anti-immigration poster', *The Telegraph*, 4 March 2009

90: Philip Mayne, The Politicisation of the Poppy: the Misuse of the Poppy by the Far Right, *Huffington Post*, 8 November 2015

91: Andrea Nill Sanchez, 'Georgia Lawmaker Defends 'Shoot To Kill' Solution To Immigration: 'They're Invading Us', *ThinkProgress*, 18 October 2010

92: Julia Rampen, 'The four most unfortunate EU-Nazi comparisons made by Brexiteers', *New Statesman*, 19 January 2017. Also, Dan Bloom 'Don't mention the war! German ambassador tells Britain to stop obsessing with the days of Churchill', *The Mirror*, 30 January 2018

93: 'Drunk bus passenger jailed over 'vile and disgusting'

racist abuse shared on Facebook, *Manchester Evening News*, 8 February 2017. See also Selina Nwulu's important essay, 'The audacity of our Skin', 6 July 2018.

94: George Fox, *Letter to Lady Claypole*, 1658 (language updated for modern English).

Chapter 9: But what would you do if ...

95: Recounted in Ruth Fry, *Victories Without Violence*, Peace Book Company, 1939

96: From Angie O'Gorman, *The Universe Bends Towards Justice: A Reader on Christian Nonviolence in the US*, New Society, 1990 reproduced in Walter Wink, *The Powers that Be*, Galilee, 1998, Chapter 8

97: Dorothy Day, *The Long Loneliness*, HarperOne, 2009

98: Assata Shakur, *An Autobiography*, Laurence Hill and co, 1987

99: Harriet Sherwood, Damien Gayle and Alice Ross, '"Hero" Imam Praises Group that Saved Finsbury Park Suspect from Angry Crowd', *The Guardian*, 19 June 2017

100: Charlotte Atler, 'The School Shooting Generation has had enough', *TIME*, 22 March 2018

About the author

Tim Gee is a writer and activist based in the UK. He has written for *The Guardian, Independent, New Internationalist* and *Peace News* amongst others. He is the author of two other books: *Counterpower: Making Change Happen* (New Internationalist, 2011) and *You Can't Evict an Idea* (Housmans, 2013). He has variously worked as a campaigner, trainer and programme developer with organisations working for human rights, global justice and the environment.

Also in this series

Quaker Roots and Branches
John Lampen

Quaker Roots and Branches explores what Quakers call their 'testimonies' – the interaction of inspiration, faith and action to bring change in the world. It looks at Quaker concerns around the sustainability of the planet, peace and war, punishment, and music and the arts in the past and today. It stresses the continuity of their witness over three hundred and sixty-five years as well as their openness to change and development.

Telling the truth about God
Rhiannon Grant

Telling the truth about God without excluding anyone is a challenge to the Quaker community. Drawing on the author's academic research into Quaker uses of religious language and her teaching to Quaker and academic groups, Rhiannon Grant aims to make accessible some key theological and philosophical insights. She explains that Quakers might sound vague but are actually making clear and creative theological claims.

What do Quakers believe?
Geoffrey Durham

Geoffrey Durham answers the crucial question 'What do Quakers believe?' clearly, straightforwardly and without jargon. In the process he introduces a unique religious group whose impact and influence in the world is far greater than their numbers suggest. *What Do Quakers Believe?* is a friendly, direct and accessible toe-in-the-water book for readers who have often wondered who these Quakers are, but have never quite found out.

CHRISTIAN ALTERNATIVE
BOOKS

THE NEW OPEN SPACES

Throughout the two thousand years of Christian tradition there
have been, and still are, groups and individuals that exist in
the margins and upon the edge of faith. But in Christianity's
contrapuntal history it has often been these outcasts and
pioneers that have forged contemporary orthodoxy out
of former radicalism as belief evolves to engage with and
encompass the ever-changing social and scientific realities. Real
faith lies not in the comfortable certainties of the Orthodox,
but somewhere in a half-glimpsed hinterland on the dirt track
to Emmaus, where the Death of God meets the Resurrection,
where the supernatural Christ meets the historical Jesus,
and where the revolution liberates both the oppressed and
the oppressors.

Welcome to Christian Alternative... a space at the edge where
the light shines through.
If you have enjoyed this book, why not tell other readers by
posting a review on your preferred book site.

Christian Atheist
Belonging without Believing
Brian Mountford
Christian Atheists don't believe in God but miss him: especially
the transcendent beauty of his music, language, ethics, and
community.
Paperback: 978-1-84694-439-0 ebook: 978-1-84694-929-6

Compassion Or Apocalypse?
A Comprehensible Guide to the Thoughts of René Girard
James Warren
How René Girard changes the way we think about God and the
Bible, and its relevance for our apocalypse-threatened world.
Paperback: 978-1-78279-073-0 ebook: 978-1-78279-072-3

Diary Of A Gay Priest
The Tightrope Walker
Rev. Dr. Malcolm Johnson
Full of anecdotes and amusing stories, but the Church is still a
dangerous place for a gay priest.
Paperback: 978-1-78279-002-0 ebook: 978-1-78099-999-9

Do You Need God?
Exploring Different Paths to Spirituality Even For Atheists
Rory J.Q. Barnes
An unbiased guide to the building blocks of spiritual belief.
Paperback: 978-1-78279-380-9 ebook: 978-1-78279-379-3

Readers of ebooks can buy or view any of these bestsellers by clicking on the live link in the title. Most titles are published in paperback and as an ebook. Paperbacks are available in traditional bookshops. Both print and ebook formats are available online.

Find more titles and sign up to our readers' newsletter at
http://www.johnhuntpublishing.com/christianity
Follow us on Facebook at
https://www.facebook.com/ChristianAlternative